AF837706

CRIMINAL PROCEDURE

CRIMINAL PROCEDURE

MODEL PROBLEMS AND OUTSTANDING ANSWERS

Carlton Bailey

Stephen M. Sheppard
SERIES EDITOR, MODEL PROBLEMS AND OUTSTANDING ANSWERS

OXFORD
UNIVERSITY PRESS

OXFORD
UNIVERSITY PRESS

Oxford University Press is a department of the University of Oxford. It furthers the University's objective of excellence in research, scholarship, and education by publishing worldwide.

Oxford New York
Auckland Cape Town Dar es Salaam Hong Kong Karachi Kuala Lumpur Madrid
Melbourne Mexico City Nairobi New Delhi Shanghai Taipei Toronto

With offices in
Argentina Austria Brazil Chile Czech Republic France Greece Guatemala Hungary
Italy Japan Poland Portugal Singapore South Korea Switzerland Thailand
Turkey Ukraine Vietnam

Oxford is a registered trademark of Oxford University Press in the UK and certain other countries.

Published in the United States of America by
Oxford University Press
198 Madison Avenue, New York, NY 10016

Library of Congress Cataloging-in-Publication Data

Bailey, Carlton, author.
Criminal procedure : model problems and outstanding answers / Carlton Bailey.
pages cm.—(Model problems and outstanding answers)
ISBN 978-0-19-979519-2 ((pbk.) : alk. paper)
1. Criminal procedure—United States—Problems, exercises, etc. I. Title.
KF9619.B35 2015
345.73'05—dc23

2014038786

Note to Readers

This publication is designed to provide accurate and authoritative information in regard to the subject matter covered. It is based upon sources believed to be accurate and reliable and is intended to be current as of the time it was written. It is sold with the understanding that the publisher is not engaged in rendering legal, accounting, or other professional services. If legal advice or other expert assistance is required, the services of a competent professional person should be sought. Also, to confirm that the information has not been affected or changed by recent developments, traditional legal research techniques should be used, including checking primary sources where appropriate.

(Based on the Declaration of Principles jointly adopted by a Committee of the American Bar Association and a Committee of Publishers and Associations.)

To my wife, soul mate and love of my life, Alberta S. Bailey,
and my special love, daughter Dr. Moya Z. Bailey,
for their love and patience, and for the love of
my wonderful mother, Nadine Walker.

CONTENTS

ABOUT THE AUTHOR

Professor Bailey is the Robert A. Leflar Professor of Law at the University of Arkansas in Fayetteville, Arkansas. Born in Fairfield, Alabama, he received a BA from Talladega College in Talladega, Alabama. After receiving a JD from the University of Chicago, he worked as a staff attorney and then the managing attorney of the Legal Aid Society in Minneapolis, Minnesota, before joining the faculty at the University of Arkansas.

Professor Bailey has focused his scholarship on criminal procedure, basic evidence, trial advocacy, and lawyering skills, and has worked with the legal clinic. He was awarded Professor of the Year in 1983 and 2014. Also, he received the University of Arkansas Alumni Award for the Outstanding Teacher in 1988. He has published a book called *Discovery Practice in Arkansas* and articles on basic evidence, criminal procedure, and discovery. He is a member of the Arkansas Supreme Court Committee on Professional Conduct and an Advisor to the Eighth Circuit Court of Appeals Advisory Committee.

PREFACE

For over ten years, I have started each of my Basic Evidence and Criminal Procedure classes with words paraphrased from the Federal Rules of Evidence 401 and 402:

> If it is relevant, then, it is admissible except if it violates the Constitution, these rules or….

Particularly in the Criminal Procedure class, we were asked to determine whether a citizen's constitutional rights were violated. Indeed, this question was consistently posed under a myriad of factual circumstances. So, in order to answer this query under these various factual settings, I invited students to help me examine and discuss the U.S. Supreme Court's interpretations (and sometimes creations) of the Fourth, Fifth, Sixth, and Fourteenth Amendments. We identified many tests and standards from those examinations and held spirited discussions. Accordingly, this book attempts to document a few of the Court's tests and standards from these four amendments.

To successfully complete this project, I am especially appreciative of the (1) outstanding secretarial assistance provided, more often under a crushing number of other office demands, by Mrs. Audrey Briggs and Ms. Jacque Fifer; and (2) unwavering support of Dean Stacy Leeds.

I also appreciate the help of Professor Steve Sheppard, William H. Enfield Professor of Law, and his trusted assistant, Paul Pellegrini.

CRIMINAL PROCEDURE

IS THE FOURTH AMENDMENT IMPLICATED? 1

OPENING REMARKS

The protections of the Fourth Amendment apply only when the government conducts a search or seizure. Although the occurrence of a search or seizure is the threshold requirement for showing that the Fourth Amendment is implicated, the U.S. Supreme Court has struggled to define a search. *Katz v. United States* held, in part, that the citizen who expects Fourth Amendment protection must, first, exhibit an actual, subjective expectation of privacy at the time and place of the search; and second, show that society recognizes this expectation of privacy as reasonable. On the other hand, the Court has recognized that some police and private conduct as *non-searches*: for example, actions (1) by a canine-sniff, (2) in an open field, (3) by private citizens, or (4) after a citizen has knowingly exposed the alleged private matter.

Another rule in *Katz* provided that what a person knowingly exposes to the public, even in his own home or office, is not a subject of Fourth Amendment protection. Similarly, the Court said in *Hoffa v. United States* that when a citizen knowingly exposes statements to others, she assumes the risk that such a person will convey the information to the police. Under such circumstances, the citizen has no reasonable expectation of privacy or she has no Fourth Amendment protection.

Knowingly Exposing

A citizen can knowingly expose something to the public in many ways. Fourth Amendment protection does not apply when a citizen makes inculpatory statements to an undercover police officer during conversations that were memorized, recorded, or simultaneously conveyed to the police, because the citizen assumed the risk that his message would be conveyed to the police. Likewise, the Court has held that a citizen has no legitimate expectation of privacy in dialed telephone numbers, because the dialed telephone numbers are knowingly exposed to the telephone company. And, when a citizen places garbage in opaque plastic bags on a public street for trash collection, the citizen assumes the risk that members of the public may gain access to its contents. Therefore, the citizen has no reasonable expectation of privacy in inculpatory items discarded in this way.

Canine-Sniff

The Supreme Court has concluded that a canine-sniff does not constitute a search because a canine-sniff is: (1) less intrusive than a typical search, (2) sui generis, and (3) so limited both in the manner in which the information is obtained and the content of the information revealed that it could not offend a reasonable privacy expectation. At the same time, the Court implied that the Fourth Amendment was not implicated when a canine-sniff disclosed only the presence or absence of a contraband item (narcotics). According to this latter interpretation, the Fourth Amendment does not protect a citizen from such a disclosure of contraband (illegal) items. Later, the Court used this same (disclosure of illegal items) reasoning to support its holding that the Fourth Amendment does not protect a citizen's expectation of privacy where either (1) the citizen's privacy interest has already been compromised by a private party's act of disclosing the container's contents, *United States v. Jacobsen*, or (2) the government agent's test to determine the nature of the item previously exposed (by the private citizen) discloses only that the item is contraband. *United States v. Jacobsen.*

The Supreme Court has also concluded that a canine-sniff conducted at either a lawful routine traffic stop or during a lawful, suspicionless checkpoint is not a search that implicates the Fourth Amendment. Indeed, some lower courts have extended to a citizen's home the rationale that a canine-sniff is not a search, despite the apparent contrary holdings in *Katz* and *Kyllo v. United States.* However, the Court has held in *Florida v. Jardines* that the police may not, without the homeowner's invitation, enter the owner's constitutionally protected area of the curtilage or his front porch in order to conduct a canine-sniff of the citizen's home. Nor, may the police unlawfully detain luggage in order to conduct a canine-sniff, *United States v. Place*.

Beeper Cases

To determine whether the government use of a beeper, a miniature battery-powered radio transmitter that emits a recurrent signal at a set frequency, is a search, a judge must decide whether the use of the beeper violated a citizen's reasonable expectation of privacy. In *United States v. Karo*, the U.S. Supreme Court held that the use of a beeper involves at least two distinct police activities—installation and monitoring, *United States v. Knotts.* For example, the Court has held that the Fourth Amendment is not implicated either (1) when a private citizen consented to allow a government agent to install a beeper into his can of ether (*United States v. Karo*), or (2) when that can of either (containing the beeper) was subsequently sold to the citizen-defendant.

Recently, however, the Supreme Court has held in *United States v. Jones* that it was an unreasonable search and seizure for the government to trespass on a citizen's car by the warrantless installation of a Global Positioning-System (GPS) tracking device on that car. And, except for a few opinions involving exigent circumstances, the government use of a beeper, without a warrant, to monitor a citizen's private residence is presumptively unreasonable under the Fourth Amendment. *United States v. Karo*.

Open Fields Doctrine

Although *Katz* specifically held that a citizen's expectation of privacy was not controlled by the place where the search occurred, the Court in *Oliver v. United States* held that a search in an open field was not protected by the Fourth Amendment. Because the Court reasoned that (1) it had held as early as 1924 that as the Fourth Amendment protected only persons, houses, papers, and effects, that protection was not extended to the open fields; and (2) a citizen's subjective, yet unreasonable, expectation of privacy in an open field was not protected under the Fourth Amendment. Still, the *Oliver* Court acknowledged that a citizen's *person, papers*, or *effects* found in an open field may be subject to Fourth Amendment protection.

Therefore, the Fourth Amendment protects a citizen or his effects, which are located in open fields, from an unreasonable search or seizure.

Despite Oliver's virtual elimination of a citizen's reasonable expectation of privacy in an open field, it did distinguish between an open field and the curtilage (area immediately surrounding the home). As a result, the extent of a citizen's Fourth Amendment protection in the curtilage is dependent on certain factors or on whether the citizen has knowingly exposed the private matter. In any event, after holding that the Fourth Amendment protected the home and its curtilage, the Court attempted to further define curtilage.

Curtilage and Flyover Cases

The Fourth Amendment protects the home and its curtilage from an unreasonable search or seizure. As noted above, "curtilage" is defined as the land immediately surrounding and associated with the home. In *United States v. Dunn,* four factors were used to determine whether it was reasonable to treat the curtilage as the home:

1. The proximity of the area claimed to be the curtilage to the home;
2. Whether the area is included within an enclosure surrounding the home;
3. The nature of the uses to which the area is put; and
4. Steps taken by the resident to protect the area from observation by people passing by.

So, whether in her house or her curtilage a citizen has no reasonable expectation of privacy if she knowingly exposes the area to the passing public or if she fails to take reasonable steps to shield her privacy from the passing public.

The U.S. Supreme Court has attempted in the aerial-surveillance cases to explain how a citizen may knowingly expose an area. First, the Court held in *Ciraolo* that the Fourth Amendment did not require the police traveling in the public airways at a lawful altitude to obtain a warrant in order to observe what is visible to the naked eye. Under these circumstances, whatever the government agents observe with the naked eye is not a *search*. In other words, the citizen has knowingly exposed the area to the flying public. Second, in a helicopter flyover case where the record did not reveal how often (or if ever) helicopters had flown over a citizen's house, a plurality of the Court in *Florida v. Riley* held that *Ciraolo* controlled. Therefore, the Fourth Amendment was not implicated as long as the officer was in lawful air space when he observed the illegal contraband with his naked eye. However, even the plurality conceded that the Fourth Amendment may be violated (1) when the inspecting officer sees intimate details connected with the use of the home or curtilage; or (2) if the helicopter causes wind, dust, or threat of injury; or (3) there is sufficient evidence that flying a helicopter is sufficiently rare in this country.

Third, five members of the *Riley* Court rejected the plurality's test for determining when an expectation of privacy is unreasonable or the citizen has knowingly exposed an area. According to five members of the Court, a citizen has not knowingly exposed an area unless there has been a showing that flying a helicopter at that altitude was sufficiently routine. Unfortunately, the justice who authored that test for a showing that the helicopter flyover must be sufficiently routine also placed the burden of making that showing on the defendant-citizen. Generally, as long as the officer was in lawful air space where any member of public could have legally passed through, then the Fourth Amendment is not implicated when an officer observes, with the naked eye, contraband in the citizen's curtilage.

HYPOTHETICAL

Police Chief Marck Jackson (hereafter "Chief Jackson") of the Fayetteberg Police Department found the following anonymous letter under his office door around 7:30 am on May 29, 2004:

> I am an employee at Wal-Market Super Center on 12th Street in Fayetteberg. You should know that several people on the Wal-Market management staff at this store are selling powdered cocaine to kids at Fayetteberg High School and Romney Jr. High. Two kids at Romney Jr. High died from overdosing on this toxic dope. The street name of this cocaine is "Triple H."
>
> By the way, some of these Wal-Market managers are quite well-known in the community. Two of them are named "Bob." You know them well! They brag on how they've made so much money selling drugs and how they can hide it through their regular jobs. They sell the cocaine from the employee restrooms at the 12th Street store. They usually sell it as *"8 balls"*—at $250 per "8 ball." They also use the employee lockers to store (and sometimes sell from) the drugs. The drugs are sometimes stored in their cars.

Chief Jackson conducted a search of police files to determine if any students from Romney Jr. High had recently died of toxic drugs. After a two-hour search he found records of three recent deaths by toxic drugs. Two of these deaths were of seventh graders at Canal Jr. High. The other death was of an eighth grader at Romney Jr. High. Chief Jackson also had several tips from reliable informants that "Bob" Sample sold drugs in the neighborhood.

After this search, Chief Jackson called the Wal-Market Home Office in Collierville. Chief Jackson identified himself and asked the appropriate personnel to locate the full name and address of the manager, "Jim Bob," at the 12th Street Super Center. After a ninety-minute search, the Home Office confirmed that there were two employee-managers at that store named "Bob." "Jim Bob" Sample was not only in his seventh year as a manager, but he was also a popular country-western singer in the Ozarks, and James Robert ("Bob") Powell was a two-year veteran and a popular thespian in a local theater troupe. "Bob" Powell, however, was on duty at a Wal-Market in China. So, Chief Jackson dispatched six officers to "Bob" Sample's home at 2342 Dayton Place.

Chief Jackson's team of six officers was led by Officer Frank Pendleton. Officer Pendleton was a ten-year veteran. When Pendleton and his team arrived at 2342 Dayton Place they discovered a bright red Aston Martin db9 automobile parked in the driveway. The vanity plates on the Aston Martin read "Bob #1". Officer Pendleton's quick computer search with the Department of Motor Vehicles revealed that the car was registered to "James Robert Sample of 2342 Dayton Place, Fayetteberg." Immediately after Officer Pendleton confirmed that "Bob" Sample was the registered owner of the db9 a man emerged from the house at 2342 Dayton Place. The man walked briskly toward the parked db9. Officer Pendleton and his fellow officers noted on their surveillance records that the man fit the description of "Bob" Sample.

"Bob" Sample entered the car, drove out of the driveway, and then north toward town. Officer Pendleton and his team of five officers followed "Bob" at a discreet distance.

Six blocks later "Bob" drove his red car to the public parking lot of the Wal-Market Store on 12th Street. When "Bob" left the car and entered the Wal-Market Store Officer Pendleton (using a laser) an undetectable laser *"print"* on the car. This invisible laser "print" allowed him to follow the car with a remote control unmanned drone aircraft (about the size of a small kite) that housed a Guardian 811 GPS tracking device. The GPS tracking device had a "live track" feature that allowed it to monitor the precise location of the *"printed"* object ("Bob" 's car) in real time. Consequently, the device made regular reports to the remote controller (Officer Pendleton) of the location, speed, and direction of "Bob's" car; the car made five extended stops for approximately three minutes each at five major intersecting streets in the city.

At each reported stop Officer Pendleton dispatched one of his officers to make an arrest of the person found at that scene. Each arrestee confessed to (moments earlier) buying drugs from "Bob" Sample. And, each arrestee possessed a small gray bag with a large triple "H" on one side and the red letters "BS" on the other side. Each gray bag contained ten (what is known in the drug vernacular) "8 balls" of powder cocaine. An "8 ball" of cocaine cost $250. All the arrestees claimed that each paid "Bob" $250.

When "Bob" Sample was subsequently arrested he was carrying $15,000 in cash, but the police did not find cocaine on his person or in his car. Moreover, a later search of his house pursuant to a warrant did not reveal any cocaine or cash. Even so, "Bob" Sample's case has been set for an arraignment and other pretrial proceedings. Sample's attorney has given us notice that he will move to suppress any and all the information collected and reported by the GPS/drone. You are an associate prosecutor. Please provide your senior prosecutor with a memorandum of law (1) analyzing the key legal precedents that the defendant will likely use to support his motions, (2) isolating the most persuasive arguments distilled from those precedents, and (3) predicting how the court is likely to rule on these competing arguments.

LIST OF READINGS

1. The Fourth Amendment to the United States Constitution.
2. Federal Rules of Evidence Rule 401. Definition of Relevant Evidence.
3. Federal Rules of Evidence Rule 402. Relevant Evidence Generally Admissible; Irrelevant Evidence Inadmissible.
4. *Olmstead v. United States*, 277 U.S. 438 (1928).
5. *Katz v. United States*, 389 U.S. 347 (1967).
6. *United States v. White*, 401 U.S. 745 (1971).
7. *Oliver v. United States*, 466 U.S. 170 (1984).
8. *United States v. Karo*, 468 U.S. 705 (1984).
9. *United States v. Knotts*, 460 U.S. 276 (1983).
10. *California v. Ciraolo*, 476 U.S. 27 (1986).
11. *Smith v. Maryland*, 442 U.S. 735 (1979).
12. *United States v. Dunn*, 480 U.S. 294 (1987).
13. *Florida v. Riley*, 486 U.S. 35 (1988).

14. Dow Chemical Co. v. United States, 476 U.S. 227 (1986), and *Dow Chemical Co. v. United States*, 749 F.2d 307 (1984).
15. *United States v. Place*, 462 U.S. 695 (1983).
16. *Illinois v. Caballes*, 543 U.S. 405 (2005).
17. *Hester v. United States*, 265 U.S. 57 (1924)
18. *California v. Greenwood*, 486 U.S. 35 (1988).
19. *United States v. Jones*, 132 S. Ct. 945 (2012).
20. *Florida v. Jardines,* 2013 U.S. Lexis 2542.
21. Peter P. Swire, Correspondence: *Katz* Is DEAD, Long Live *Katz*, 102 Mich. L. Rev. 904 (2004).
22. Stephen A. Saltzburg, *Another Victim of Illegal Narcotics: The Fourth Amendment (as Illustrated by the Open Fields Doctrine*, 48 U. Pitt. L. Rev. 1 (1986).
23. 1 W. LaFave, Search and Seizure § 2.1(d), pp. 393–94 (3d ed. 1996).
24. Leslie A. Lunney, "Has the Fourth Amendment Gone to the Dogs? Unreasonable Expansion of Canine Sniff Doctrine to Include Sniff of the Home," 88 Or. L. Rev. 832–42 (2009).

SAMPLE ESSAY

To: Senior Prosecutor
From: Associate Prosecutor
Re: Suppression Hearing—[*State v. Sample*]
Defendant's motion to exclude information from GPS device
Date:

In response to the motions-in-limine by the defendant that are described above, I have prepared the following memorandum of law for your consideration. As you will discover this memorandum attempts to (1) identify the key legal precedents that the defendant has asserted to support his motions under the facts set out below, (2) isolate the most persuasive arguments distilled from these precedents that he has asserted (and our counterarguments to them), and (3) predict how the court is likely to rule on these competing arguments.

Essentially, the defendant argues that his Fourth Amendment rights were violated when the police conducted a warrantless search and seizure by laser "printing" his car, which allowed Pendleton to track his car with a GPS tracking device and then using that device to monitor that car's movements on public streets. The defendant claims that the fruits of this alleged unreasonable search and seizure were used to identify and arrest him and others for allegedly violating applicable laws against trafficking in controlled substances. Therefore the defendant argues that the location and information from the arrestee is tainted and thereby subject to exclusion as fruits of the poisonous tree.

Although the holding in *United States v. Jones* may appear to support the defendant's argument that the warrantless printing and monitoring of his car with a GPS tracking device violates the Fourth Amendment, *Jones* specifically acknowledges that under certain circumstances such *warrantless* use of a GPS device may not violate the Fourth Amendment. According to the *Jones, United States v. Knotts* is still good law. That is, a citizen's reasonable expectation of privacy has not been infringed where the information obtained by the government's use of an enhancement device merely reveals the location of a citizen's automobile at some public place. Our argument is based squarely on *United States v. Knotts* and *United States v. Jones* because the Fourth Amendment is not violated where the GPS tracking device provides only public information. Accordingly, the trial court must decide if *Knotts* and *Jones* are dispositive.

PART A. THE GENERAL RULE OF ADMISSIBILITY

Federal Rule of Evidence 401 provides that all relevant evidence is admissible except as otherwise provided by the Constitution of the United States. Because the Fourth Amendment to the United States Constitution prohibits unreasonable searches and seizures, any unreasonable search or seizure violates the Fourth Amendment. For example, the Supreme Court has held that a warrantless search by a government agent that interferes with a citizen's reasonable expectation of privacy violates the Fourth Amendment protection of a citizen's property. *Katz v. United States*. More important, in order to make this Fourth Amendment protection effective the Supreme Court has held that evidence seized as a result of the unlawful search cannot constitute proof, at trial, against the victim of the search. *Wong Sun v. United States*, 371 U.S. 471, 484–88 (1963); *Mapp v. Ohio*, 367 U.S. 643 (1961).

At the pretrial proceeding, the judge must determine whether *United States v. Knotts*, 460 U.S. 276 (1983), or *United States v. Jones*, 132 S. Ct. 945 (2012), controls the facts of our case.

PART B. POLICE USE OF A GPS DEVICE = *SEARCH*?

At the suppression hearing we should expect the defendants to contend that the Fourth Amendment was implicated when the police used the GPS device on citizen Sample's automobile. The defendant will claim that by using the GPS device on Sample's automobile the police conducted a warrantless search of his car. *United States v. Jones*, 132 S. Ct. 945 (2012). A warrantless search, they will argue, is presumptively unreasonable under the Fourth Amendment. Accordingly, information obtained by exploiting this unreasonable search becomes the tainted fruit of the poisonous tree. And as the police used this tainted information to collect further incriminating evidence against Sample, this additional evidence is tainted and therefore excludable pursuant to the exclusionary rule. *Weeks v. United States*, 232 U.S. 33 (1914); *Mapp v. Ohio*, 367 U.S. 643 (1961).

The key to the defendant's argument under *United States v. Jones* is that a majority of the Court determined that the government's act of installing a GPS tracking device on the defendant's car without a warrant was a trespass on a protected area ("affect") enumerated in the Fourth Amendment. In *Jones*, the Court announced: "We hold that the government's installation of a GPS device on a target's vehicle, and its use of that device to monitor the vehicle's movements, constitutes a search." Although this language is quite precise the *Jones* Court does not command a finding of a Fourth Amendment violation under our facts because the government did not trespass on the citizen's car, and the evidence obtained from the GPS tracking device was only public information.

More important, the defendant's reliance on *United States v. Jones* is misplaced. The *Jones* Court emphasized that its decision in *Katz v. United States* created two tests for determining whether the Fourth Amendment was implicated. That is, the *Katz* reasonable-expectation-of-privacy test has been added to, not substituted for, the common-law trespassory test. Under our facts the government's use of the GPS tracking device is not a search under either test. If there is no search then the Fourth Amendment does not apply. And if the Fourth Amendment does not apply, there can be no Fourth Amendment violation.

First, under *Katz*'s reasonable-expectation-of-privacy test, the defendant did not exhibit an actual, subjective expectation of privacy. Besides, an expectation that the government would not use a laser beam to print the exterior of one's car to facilitate the use of a GPS device is unreasonable. Activities that the defendant knowingly exposes to the plain view of outsiders are not protected because no intention to keep them to himself has been exhibited.

Second, the *Jones*' Court requirement of a trespass did not occur under our facts.

TOOLS FOR SELF-CRITICISM

Determining whether our facts are controlled by *United States v. Knotts* or *United States v. Jones* is not as clear as the prosecutor's essay suggests because neither *Knotts* nor *Jones* precisely address the facts in our scenario. Indeed, *Jones* acknowledged that the *Knotts* holding was still viable. That is, the Fourth Amendment does not protect a citizen from the government's use of a device that produces only public information. However, the *Jones* Court also recognized that *Knotts* left one matter unresolved. *Knotts* noted the limited use that the government made of the signals from this particular beeper and reserved the question whether different constitutional principles may be applicable to dragnet-type law enforcement practices of the type that GPS tracking made possible here.

Although the GPS tracking device was used in a limited way under our facts it is not certain that even without a trespass the Fourth Amendment may be implicated. Our facts disclose that the government did place a laser print on the car in order to track it. Even so, this is neither collecting information from a citizen solely by observation nor is it an act of installing the laser print on the car. Indeed, the concurrence in *Jones* reasoned that those two options should not be controlling. Whether the surveillance time was an extended period as in *Jones* or brief period as in *Katz*, the concurrence argued that the electronic or other novel modes of surveillance do not depend upon a physical invasion on property. A search should be determined, according to the concurrence, by the transmission of electronic signals and the unique attributes of the surveillance system as defined in *Katz*. Unfortunately, the concurrence failed to discuss the *Katz* precondition: a reasonable expectation of privacy.

THE FOURTH AMENDMENT—SENSE-ENHANCING DEVICES, PROBABLE CAUSE, AND THE GOOD FAITH EXCEPTION

2

OPENING REMARKS

The Fourth Amendment is implicated when a search or seizure occurs. The Supreme Court has struggled to define a search, particularly when it had to evaluate the impact of a sense-enhancing device. For example, the Court has held that the government's use of a sense-enhancing device is not a search where the government conducted a warrantless (1) canine-sniff of (a) luggage briefly detained at an airport; or (b) a car lawfully stopped, and (2) aerial surveillance of a chemical manufacturing plant with a precision aerial mapping camera.

On the other hand, the Court has guarded a citizen's privacy interests more closely by holding that an unconstitutional search occurred when the government either trespassed on the citizen's property (car) to install GPS tracking device, *United States v. Jones*, or used a device that (1) intruded on a citizen's constitutionally protected area (telephone booth), *Katz v. United States*, or (2) revealed information about the citizen's home that would not have been available without entering the home, *United States v. Karo* and *Kyllo v. United States*. Indeed, in 2013, the Court held in *Florida v. Jardines* that the police may not, without the homeowner's invitation, enter the owner's constitutionally protected area of the curtilage or his front porch in order to conduct a canine-sniff of the citizen's home.

Kyllo—The Use of Sense-Enhancing Technology on the Home

Kyllo asked whether a search had occurred when the police used a sense-enhancing device (thermal imager) to search a citizen's house. The majority's answer was a problematic yes. The Court acknowledged that the *Katz* test defined the search of a telephone booth, automobiles, or the curtilage. However, the interior of a home, the Court instructs, is guaranteed a minimal expectation of privacy under the Fourth Amendment. Pursuant to this view it is unnecessary to conduct a *Katz* analysis to determine whether an expectation of privacy is due. As a result, if the government was allowed to use a sense-enhancing device, without a warrant, on a citizen's home, such an act would erode that privacy guaranteed by the Fourth Amendment.

The test crafted by the *Kyllo* Court provides that a search has occurred when the government uses sense-enhancing technology, that is not in general use by the public, on a citizen's home without a warrant, and extracts any information regarding the interior of the home that could not otherwise have been obtained without a physical intrusion into that constitutionally protected area. Any search conducted without a warrant is presumptively unreasonable under the Fourth Amendment. And, an unreasonable search is a violation of the Fourth Amendment. Accordingly, if the government uses sense- enhancing technology, that is not in general use by the public, to perform a search without a warrant, any evidence derived from this presumptively unreasonable search is a (tainted) fruit of the poisonous tree. Such fruits are required to be excluded pursuant to the exclusionary rule.

Kyllo provides, however, that even if a trial court is required to exclude evidence because of a Fourth Amendment violation, the court may admit the evidence if the court determines that the search warrant was supported by probable cause untainted by the police use of that sense-enhancing device. Consequently, the trial court may find that the warrant is not defective if probable cause is supported by the remaining untainted facts in the affidavit to the warrant. Even if the warrant proves defective, the trial court may circumvent the exclusionary rule by finding a good faith exception to the warrant requirement. In order to complete the legal resources necessary for our analysis, an examination of probable cause, the exclusionary rule, and its good faith exception is required. Each matter will be discussed in the order presented.

Another Basis for Probable Cause

The general definition for probable cause when based on an officer's own observations is: if the facts and circumstances before the officer are such as to warrant a man of prudence and caution believing that the offense has been committed, it is sufficient. In other words, what did the officer know? And, when did he know it? After this early interpretation two notable opinions continued to employ this general definition—*Carroll v. United States* and *Brinegar v. United States.*

CARROLL V. UNITED STATES

The holding in *Carroll* was the genesis for the so-called automobile-exception to the warrant requirement. This exception has been described as the reasonableness of the police to conduct a warrantless search of a vehicle stopped on the open road because it could be quickly moved out of the location where the warrant must be sought. Probable cause as to an automobile or the *Carroll* automobile-exception does not apply to our hypothetical. *Carroll* will be examined more particularly with the other automobile-exception cases.

BRINEGAR V. UNITED STATES

Brinegar provides a list of long-standing measures that courts have used to describe, explain, or otherwise define probable cause as: (1) more than base suspicion; (2) being about probabilities (probabilities are not technical; they are the factual and practical considerations of everyday life on which reasonable and prudent men, not legal technicians, act); (3) reasonably arising out of circumstances, known to the seizing officer, that an automobile or other vehicle contains that which by law is subject to seizure and destruction; (4) contemplating individualized focus on a citizen or his automobile (that is, the police may not stop all citizens or all cars); (5) not requiring the use of the rules of evidence for deciding probable cause; and (5) distinguishing the nature and mode of proof required to establish probable cause as substantially different from the proof required to establish the guilt of a defendant at trial.

Generally, a warrantless search of a car or the warrantless seizure of a person is reasonable under the Fourth Amendment when that search or seizure is based on sufficient facts personally known to the officer (probable cause) conducting the search or seizure. This general rule does not apply if the warrantless search or seizure is conducted by an officer who lacks personal knowledge of sufficient facts, but merely suspects or believes evidence may be found or a crime may have been committed, unless the officer receives his information from a third-party informant.

The General Test Compared to *Illinois v. Gates* and Third-Party Based Probable Cause

The U.S. Supreme Court has held that a warrant was void if the affiant-government agent made assertions in the affidavit (supporting the warrant request) that *contained no facts upon which to base a finding of probable cause.* Assertions in an affidavit that merely affirms a *belief* or a *suspicion* are insufficient to support probable cause to search a private dwelling. Not only has the Court prohibited the affiant-government agent from using mere assertions of *belief* or *suspicion* to establish probable cause, but her third-party informant is similarly restricted.

To establish probable cause based on an *informant's tip, the informer's report* must (according to *Aguilar/Spinelli*) show (1) he is a reliable or truthful informant, (2) that his report is based on sufficient facts *(basis in knowledge),* or that his report has been sufficiently corroborated; or (3) specifically detailed (suggesting that it was reliably received), or (4) the rest of the affidavit shows that something alleged permits the suspicion engendered by the informant's report to ripen into probable cause.

Gates overruled the test used in *Aguilar/Spinelli*, and replaced it with a totality-of-the-circumstances test. According to *Gates,* the totality test was more flexible and more easily applied than the rigid *Aguilar/Spinelli* approach. Even though *Aguilar/Spinelli* appears as flexible as *Gates*, there are some notable differences. Unlike *Aguilar/Spinelli, Gates* adopts the totality-of-the-circumstances approach as the dispositive way for determining all probable cause issues; it allows a court to determine probable cause solely on the reliability of the informant. Moreover, the Supreme Court has specifically emphasized that it rejected the *Aguilar/Spinelli* test in *Massachusetts v. Upton*. That is, an affidavit supporting probable cause for a search warrant should be looked at in its entirety, not by judging bits and pieces in isolation against the artificial standards provided by the *Aguilar/Spinelli* test. Similarly the Court has adopted de novo review for probable cause determinations to, in part, allow appellate courts to maintain control of, and to clarify, the legal principles in the totality-of-the-circumstances test.

Probable Cause—How Specific

From the beginning the Supreme Court has condemned writs of assistance and general warrants as violations of the Fourth Amendment's particularity requirement. The Court has held that this particularity requirement applies to persons as well as to places. In the words of the Court, "[w]here the standard is probable cause, a search or seizure of a person must be supported by probable cause particularized with respect to that person." *Ybarra v. Illinois*. Nevertheless, the Court has recently held that the police had probable cause under the Fourth Amendment to arrest anyone or all three men (stopped in a car) for possession of illegal drugs and cash found in that car. The Court concluded that unlike a patron in a public tavern *(Ybarra),* passengers in a car will often be engaged in a common enterprise with the driver. Consequently, the Court opined that where the guilty person is not singled out by anyone (one of the other occupants in the car)

> It was reasonable for the officer to infer a common enterprise among the three men. The quantity of drugs and cash in the car indicated the likelihood of drug dealing, an enterprise to which a dealer would be unlikely to admit an innocent person with the potential to furnish evidence against him. *Maryland v. Pringle*, 540 U.S. 366, 373 (2003).

Even where a court determines that a warrant was void or the police lacked probable cause to conduct a search or seizure, the remedy of exclusion may not be available to a defendant.

The Exclusionary Rule and Its Good Faith Exception

In *Wong Sun v. United States*, the Supreme Court held, among other things, that where incriminating evidence against the accused is discovered by the unconstitutional actions of the police, in order to determine whether to exclude the incriminating evidence, a court must decide

> Whether granting establishment of the primary illegality, the evidence to which instant objection is made has been come at by exploitation of that illegality or instead by means sufficiently distinguishable to be purged of the primary taint.

Pursuant to *Wong Sun*, the *taint* of the unconstitutional police conduct may be removed or purged through a process called *attenuation*. If the *taint* is removed, the incriminating evidence may be admitted into evidence against the accused. *Wong Sun* defined *attenuation*:

> Attenuation can occur, of course, when the casual connection is remote… [or] the interest protected by the constitutional guarantee that has been violated would not be served by suppression of the evidence obtained.

Early in its history, the Court held that where the government compels a citizen to produce evidence of wrongdoing and subsequently admits the compelled evidence, these actions, taken together, violate a citizen's Fourth and Fifth Amendments rights. Although the Court did not used the term "exclusionary rule," by stitching the Fourth and Fifth Amendments together in this way, the Court created an exclusionary rule. Subsequent to this early interpretation, however, the Court's interpretation of its exclusionary rule has not, except for a few notable exceptions (*Ker v. California, Mapp v. Ohio*), used the rationale that the Fourth and Fifth Amendments run almost into each other. Instead, the Court has either implied a rationale or explicitly identified alternative rationales for the exclusionary rule.

THE GOOD FAITH EXCEPTION TO THE EXCLUSIONARY RULE

In 1984, the Supreme Court in *United States v. Leon* explained that it had adopted a deterrence-based theory for determining whether the exclusionary rule should be imposed. That means a court had to evaluate the costs and benefits to the adversarial system before imposing the exclusionary remedy.

The Court noted that the exclusionary rule could be modified by adopting a good faith exception without jeopardizing the rule's ability to perform its intended function. More specifically, the Court stated that suppressing evidence obtained pursuant to a warrant should be ordered only on a case-by-case basis and then only in unusual cases where exclusion would further the purposes of the exclusionary rule. The Court explained that in order for the exclusionary rule to have any deterrent effect, it must alter the behavior of individual law enforcement officers or the policies of their departments. Similarly, the good faith exception may apply even where the police have acted negligently. As a result, violation of the Fourth Amendment does not necessarily result in the exclusion of the evidence. According to the Court, where the police error was merely negligent but neither reckless nor deliberate, the error is not enough by itself to require the extreme sanction of exclusion.

Based on this reasoning, the Court concluded that exclusion is not a necessary consequence of a Fourth Amendment violation. Instead, the Court focused on the efficacy of the rule in deterring Fourth Amendment violations in the future. However, the Court warned the government that judges may be deterred and suppression may be an appropriate remedy where (1) the judge issuing the warrant was misled by information in an affidavit that the affiant knew was false or should have known was false except for his reckless disregard of the truth, (2) the issuing magistrate wholly abandoned her neutral and detached function (a rubber stamp for the police), (3) an officer relied on a warrant based on an affidavit so lacking in indicia of probable cause as to render official belief in its existence entirely unreasonable, (4) depending on the circumstances, a warrant was so facially deficient—that is, in failing to particularize the place to be searched or the things to be seized—that the executing officers could not reasonably presume it to be valid; (5) the magistrate's probable cause determination reflected an improper analysis of the totality of the circumstances, or (6) sufficient information was not presented to the judge and the judge determined probable cause by ratifying the bare conclusions of others.

HYPOTHETICAL

Police Chief Marck Jackson ("Chief Jackson") of the Fayetteberg Police Department found the following anonymous letter under his office door around 7:30 am on May 29, 2004:

> I am an employee at Wal-Market Super Center on 12th Street in Fayetteberg. You should know that several people on the Wal-Market management staff at this store are selling powdered cocaine to kids at Fayetteberg High School and Romney Jr. High. Two kids at Romney Jr. High died from overdosing on this toxic dope. The street name of this cocaine is "Triple H."
>
> By the way, some of these Wal-Market managers are quite well-known in the community. Two of them are named "Bob." You know them well! They brag on how they've made so much money selling drugs and how they can hide it through their

regular jobs. They sell the cocaine from the employee restrooms at the 12th Street store. They also use the employee lockers to store (and sometimes sell from) the drugs. The drugs are sometimes stored in their cars.

Chief Jackson conducted a search of police files to determine if any students from Romney Jr. High had recently died of toxic drugs. After a two-hour search he found records of three recent deaths by toxic drugs. Two of these deaths were of seventh graders at Canal Jr. High. The other death was of an eighth grader at Romney Jr. High. Chief Jackson also had several tips from reliable informants that "Bob" Sample sold drugs in the neighborhood.

After this search, Chief Jackson called the Wal-Market Home Office in Collierville. Chief Jackson identified himself and asked the appropriate personnel to locate the full name and address of the manager, "Jim Bob," at the 12th Street Super Center. After a ninety-minute search, the Home Office confirmed that there were two employee-managers at that store named "Bob." "Jim Bob" Sample was not only in his seventh year as a manager, but he was also a popular country-western singer in the Ozarks; James Robert ("Bob") Powell was a two-year veteran and a popular thespian in a local theater troupe. "Bob" Powell, however, was on duty at a Wal-Market in China. So, Chief Jackson dispatched six officers to "Bob" Sample's home at 2342 Dayton Place.

Chief Jackson's team of six officers was led by Officer Frank Pendleton, a ten-year veteran. When Pendleton and his team arrived at 2342 Dayton Place they discovered that they could not observe, from ground level, a greenhouse located in the backyard of the property, nor could they see any other aspects of the house. They were not able to see any exterior details of the house or the greenhouse because the property was totally enclosed by a ten-foot-high oak paneled fence that had several "DO NOT ENTER" signs written in red ink posted at each corner. Despite these obstacles Officer Pendleton persevered. Indeed, he was able to view (and record the license plate number) of all the people who drove up to, entered, and exited the metal-and-oak door built into the ten-foot oak fence. His written report (and the subsequent affidavit) noted that this door had an obvious peephole in its center. During a two-hour observation period Officer Pendleton and his team of officers observed and noted at least seven cars drive up to the metal-and-oak door. Although each car contained several occupants, only the occupant in the front passenger seat emerged and entered through the door.

All the visitors were young men between twenty and thirty years. Half of the *visitors* were either Hispanic or African-American. The rest were white. Each *visitor* was observed (and noted) knocking twice on the door while he cautiously looked up and down the street. Immediately the door would open and the *visitor* would quickly enter. As the *visitor* began to enter the door would begin to close. Consequently, after the *visitor* entered the door would instantly close behind him. After a minute or less the door would reopen and the *visitor* hurriedly emerged carrying a small brown paper bag. Then the *visitor* would leap into the waiting car and quickly drive away. One of the seven *visitors* was recognized by Officer Pendleton as a known drug user: "Snow Ball" (a white male about six feet tall).

Officer Pendleton requested of and received permission from the police department to use the newly developed Millivision (radar) binoculars, which were on loan from the Federal Bureau of Investigation (FBI). The newly developed Millivision

("Millys") binoculars were capable of seeing through fences (metal wood, rock), heavy brush, or walls. The binoculars allowed the user to see the outline of persons, objects in their hands or on their body, body parts, and any items underneath their clothing.

Officer Pendleton and his team assumed positions in two squad cars approximately one hundred yards from 2342 Dayton Place. Although he had the aid of the binoculars, and although he could see through the fence, except for an exchange of a brown paper bag for something "paperlike" in the hands of each *"visitor"* he could not see any other activity. Officer Pendleton turned the focus of the "Millys" on "Bob" Sample's house. The officer could "see through" the walls of the upstairs rooms. Through the "Millys" he was able to see two people (a man and a woman) in a second- floor bedroom. Moreover, he could see through the clothes both were wearing. On the male figure he could see a package shaped in the (based on his experience) well-known cocaine bow tie taped to the small of the male figure's back. After getting out of the car and moving to the partially see-through gate door, Officer Pendleton could see through the walls at the first-floor level. Here he saw one marijuana plant in Sample's first-floor hall closet. And he saw sixty bags of powder substance he thought to be cocaine.

Armed with (1) the anonymous letter; (2) the "findings" of Chief Jackson's investigation; (3) the surveillance observations regarding the seven *"visitors,"* and (4) the information disclosed through use of the "Millys," Officer Pendleton secured a search warrant to search "Bob" Sample's residence and greenhouse area. Officer Pendleton knocked three times on the front door as he announced in a loud voice, "Police, we're here to conduct a search of the premises." Officer Pendleton was accompanied by eight officers. Simultaneously twelve other officers approached the back door to the Sample house and the greenhouse nearby. Before Sample could answer the knock on his door, Officer Pendleton and his team entered the house. Five pounds of cocaine were lying openly on Sample's coffee table. Sample and his lady friend (Chancé James) were arrested. Both were searched. A pound of cocaine was found attached to Sample's back. James had thirty freshly rolled "blunts" (marijuana wrapped) in her purse. One marijuana plant was found in the first floor closet, and sixty bags of cocaine were found in the nearby greenhouse.

Bob Sample and James have hired lawyers. An arraignment has been set. At that arraignment Sample and James will request that all of the evidence be suppressed. You are an associate prosecutor. Please provide your senior prosecutor with a memorandum of law: (1) analyzing the key legal precedents that the defendants will likely use to support their motions, (2) isolating the most persuasive arguments distilled from those precedents, and (3) predicting how the court is likely to rule on these competing arguments.

LIST OF READINGS

1. The Fourth Amendment to the United States Constitution.
2. Federal Rules of Evidence Rule 401. Definition of Relevant Evidence.
3. Federal Rules of Evidence Rule 402. Relevant Evidence Generally Admissible; Irrelevant Evidence Inadmissible.
4. *Boyd v. United States*, 116 U.S. 616 (1886).
5. *Katz v. United States*, 389 U.S. 347 (1967).

6. *United States v. Karo*, 468 U.S. 705 (1984).
7. *United States v. Knotts*, 460 U.S. 276 (1983).
8. *Dow Chemical Co. v. United States*, 476 U.S. 227 (1986).
9. *Kyllo v. United States*, 533 U.S. 27 (2001).
10. *Wong Sun v. United States*, 371 U.S. 471 (1963).
11. *Franks v. Delaware*, 438 U.S. 154 (1978).
12. *Stacey v. Emery*, 97 U.S. 642 (1878).
13. *Carroll v. United States*, 267 U.S. 132 (1925).
14. *Brinegar v. United States*, 338 U.S. 160 (1949).
15. *Nathanson v. United States*, 290 U.S. 41 (1933).
16. *Illinois v. Gates*, 462 U.S. 213 (1983).
17. *Aguilar v. Texas*, 378 U.S. 108 (1964).
18. *Spinelli v. United States*, 393 U.S. 40 (1969).
19. *Draper v. United States*, 358 U.S. 307 (1959).
20. *Mapp v. Ohio*, 367 U.S. 643 (1961).
21. *Weeks v. United States*, 232 U.S. 383 (1914).
22. *Burdeau v. McDowell*, 256 U.S. 465 (1921).
23. *Massachusetts v. Sheppard*, 468 U.S. 981 (1984).
24. *Leon v. United States*, 468 U.S. 897 (1984).
25. *Hudson v. Michigan*, 547 U.S. 586 (2006).
26. *Ornelas v. United States*, 517 U.S. 690 (1996).
27. *Ybarra v. Illinois*, 444 U.S. 85 (1979).
28. *Maryland v. Pringle*, 540 U.S. 366 (2003).
29. *Herring v. United States*, 555 U.S. 135 (2009).
30. *Giordenello v. United States*, 357 U.S. 480 (1958).
31. *Florida v. Jardines*, 2013 U.S. Lexis 2542.
32. Yale Kamisar, Does (Did) (Should) the Exclusionary Rule Rest on a "Principled Basis" Rather than an "Empirical Proposition"? 16 Creighton L. Rev. 565, 627–45 (1983).
33. Orin S. Kerr, The Fourth Amendment and New Technologies: Constitutional Myths and the Case for Creation, 102 Mich. L. Rev. 709 (2004).
34. Peter P. Swire, Correspondence: *Katz* Is DEAD, Long Live *Katz*, 102 Mich. L. Rev. 904 (2004).
35. Ronald J. Allen et al, Criminal Procedure, Investigation and Right to Counsel, P.3 § C.1 The Probable Cause Standard 429 (2005).

SAMPLE ESSAY

To: Senior Prosecutor
From: Associate Prosecutor
Re: Suppression Hearing—[*State v. Sample and James*]
Defendants' motions to exclude cocaine and marijuana plants seized pursuant to a warrant and a search incident to an arrest
Date:

In anticipation of the forthcoming motions-in-limine by the defendants that are described above, I have prepared the following memorandum of law for your consideration. As you will discover this memorandum attempts to (1) identify the key legal precedents that the defendants will use to support their likely motions under the facts set out below, (2) isolate the most persuasive arguments distilled from these precedents that they are likely to assert (and our counterarguments to them), and (3) predict how the court is likely to rule on these competing arguments.

Essentially, the defendants will argue that their Fourth Amendment rights were violated when the police conducted a warrantless search and seizure by employing a sense-enhancing device on their home. *Kyllo v. United States*, 533 U.S. 27 (2001). The defendants will claim that the fruits of that unreasonable (warrantless) search and seizure were used in an affidavit to secure a search warrant for their home. Next, the defendants will argue that all of the illegal drugs found pursuant to that search warrant are tainted and thereby subject to exclusion as fruits of the poisonous tree.

Although the holding in *Kyllo* provides that the government use of a sense-enhancing device that is not in general use by the public is a search, and evidence seized from such a search may be excluded. *Kyllo* recognizes two exceptions to this rule of exclusion—probable cause sustainable with information gleaned from a source other than that from the sense-enhancing device, and the good faith exception to the exclusionary rule. *United States v. Leon*, 468 U.S. 897.

PART A. THE GENERAL RULE OF ADMISSIBILITY

Federal Rule of Evidence 401 provides that all relevant evidence is admissible "… except as *otherwise* provided by the Constitution of the United States… " Because the Fourth Amendment to the United States Constitution prohibits unreasonable searches and seizures, any unreasonable search or seizure violates the Fourth Amendment. For example, the Supreme Court has held that a warrantless search by a government agent, which interfered with a citizen's reasonable expectation of privacy, violates the Fourth Amendment. *Katz v. United States*, 389 U.S. 347 (1967). More important, in order to make this Fourth Amendment protection effective, the Supreme Court has held that evidence seized as a result of the unlawful search could not constitute proof at trial against the victim of the search.

At the pretrial process, the judge must determine whether

(a) The police use of that sense-enhancing device was a warrantless search;
(b) That warrantless search was reasonable;
(c) The information gleaned via the enhancing device was necessary to support probable
cause for that search warrant, and
(d) the good faith exception to the search warrant applies even if the warrant lacked probable cause.

PART B. POLICE USE OF A SENSE-ENHANCING DEVICE = *SEARCH*

At the suppression hearing we should expect the defendants to contend that the Fourth Amendment was implicated when the police used the Millivision binoculars to see through the walls of the defendant's house. The defendants will claim that by using the binoculars in this way the police conducted a warrantless search of the house. A warrantless search, they will argue, is presumptively unreasonable under the Fourth Amendment. Accordingly, information obtained by exploiting this unreasonable search becomes the tainted fruit of the poisonous tree. And, as the police used this tainted information in an affidavit to establish probable cause for a search warrant, the resulting search warrant was invalid. As a result, they will argue that all the evidence seized pursuant to this invalid warrant should be excluded pursuant to the exclusionary rule. Although the defendants may persuade the judge that the police use of the binoculars was a warrantless search under the Fourth Amendment, it is very unlikely that they can show that the search warrant was invalid due to a lack of probable cause.

Despite the defendants' arguments and conclusion we can successfully show that our search warrant was based on probable cause. Hence, the evidence seized pursuant to that search warrant is lawful and admissible. According to *Kyllo* the state is allowed to show that our search warrant was based on probable cause even if the information obtained via the enhanced technology is excludable under the exclusionary rule. Moreover, our successful showing is not compromised by conceding that (1) the police acquired part of the information to support probable cause in the warrant from the warrantless use of enhanced technology, (2) the enhanced technology used was not in general public use, (3) the use of this enhanced technology allowed the police to obtain information from the interior of the defendant's home that could not otherwise have been acquired, and (4) as a consequence the warrantless use of the enhanced technology under these circumstances constituted an unreasonable search.

So, even where the state has obtained information used to support probable cause for a search warrant through an unreasonable search and seizure, *Kyllo* allows the state to save the validity of the search warrant by showing the court that the unlawfully acquired information was unnecessary to establish probable cause:

> Without the evidence it provided, the search warrant issued in this case was supported by probable cause… and if not, whether there is any other basis for supporting admission of the evidence that the search pursuant to the warrant produced.

In this case Officer Pendleton's use of the information disclosed through the enhanced technology, the binoculars, constituted only a part of the information used to support probable cause. Indeed, the search warrant was secured by presenting the judge with information of (1) the anonymous letter, (2) the findings of Chief Jackson's investigation, (3) the surveillance observations regarding the seven visitors to the defendant's house, and (4) the information disclosed through the enhanced technology. Under current law the judge at the suppression hearing must evaluate an affidavit supporting probable cause for a search warrant consistent with the *Illinois v. Gates* totality-of-the-circumstances test by looking at the affidavit in its entirety, not judging bits and pieces in isolation against artificial standards. Based on our facts there is sufficient support for the judge to find probable cause without using the information from the enhanced technology.

TOOLS FOR SELF-CRITICISM

The question presented *and* the answer offered are based on applicable legal precedents. The second paragraph of the essay provides that the state police will be accused of violating the defendants' Fourth Amendment rights by conducting a warrantless search and seizure by employing a sense-enhancing device on their home. Furthermore the defendants will argue that because this warrantless search is presumptively unreasonable under the Fourth Amendment any fruits (information) obtained and subsequently used to secure a search warrant should result in an unconstitutional warrant. Accordingly, the defendants will maintain that all the contraband (cocaine, etc.) seized pursuant to this alleged unconstitutional warrant should be excluded as fruits of the poisonous tree. Contrary to the defendants' arguments we should successfully rebut these arguments pursuant to *Kyllo*.

Although the holding in *Kyllo* provides that the police's warrantless use of a sense-enhancing device ("that is not in general use by the public") is a search, and that evidence *seized* during such a search may be excluded, *Kyllo* recognizes two exceptions to this rule of exclusion: probable cause is sustainable without the information gleaned from the police's use of a warrantless sense-enhancing device, and the good faith exception to the exclusionary rule applies. Regrettably, the Court did not fully define the first potential exception ("probable cause sustainable without… "), and the second (good faith exception) appears to be limited to special facts.

> Officer Rombach's application for a warrant clearly was supported by much more than a "bare bones" affidavit. The affidavit related the results of an extensive investigation and, as the opinions of the divided panel of the Court of Appeals make clear, provided evidence sufficient to create disagreement among thoughtful and competent judges to the existence of probable cause. Under these circumstances…

468 U.S. at 926. Consequently, we will have the burden of showing that the magistrate could find that a fair probability existed under the totality of the remaining (after the information from the sense-enhancing device was deleted) circumstances to establish probable cause. As the *Kyllo* Court did not explain this exception we will have to educate the judge on how this exception should work. We are aided in this effort by a Supreme Court opinion *(Franks v. Delaware)*, which allows a citizen to attack the veracity of a warrant affidavit. Indeed, in a case where a policeman has intentionally falsified information to establish probable cause the Court has held, in part, that the warrant is not presumptively invalid. A warrant (issued by a neutral magistrate) is presumptively valid. Still, a showing by an aggrieved citizen that the warrant was obtained by false statements from the officer may entitle that citizen to a hearing on that issue. Moreover, to be entitled to a hearing the citizen must identify specific portions of the warrant containing deliberately false statements. Even if a judge accepts the false statements as true the judge is also allowed to set the false statement to one side (does not consider them as facts supporting the warrant) when considering the remaining facts; if the judge finds that there remains sufficient content in the warrant affidavit to support a finding of probable cause, no hearing is required. Besides, even if the citizen persuades a judge to convene a hearing, whether the citizen will prevail at that hearing is, of course, another issue.

Although it is not clearly defined, *Kyllo*'s exception of allowing a court to determine probable cause on the basis of the remaining non-sense-enhanced information (in an affidavit) is consistent with the other Supreme Court precedent (*Franks v. Delaware*). Indeed, the Court has held that even where a showing has been made that an affidavit for a warrant contains deliberate falsehoods or statements that display a reckless disregard for the truth, a judge may still find that an affidavit supports probable cause; that is, if the deliberate falsehoods are set to one side and there remains sufficient content in the warrant affidavit to support a finding of probable cause, there is no Fourth Amendment violation.

VARIATIONS ON A THEME

The central theme of the hypothetical is the legality of a warrant based on information obtained, in part, from the police's warrantless use of a sense-enhancing device (that was not in general public use). Clearly such a warrant is not invalid if the remaining information in the affidavit supports probable cause. However, even if the remaining information does not support probable cause, the prosecutor may successfully argue under the facts of our case that the good faith exception to the exclusionary rule preserves the seized evidence for trial.

THE WARRANT PROCESS, KNOCK AND ANNOUNCE, PLAIN VIEW

3

OPENING REMARKS

The Warrant Requirement

The Supreme Court has extensively emphasized the Fourth Amendment's second clause, which provides that no warrants shall issue, but upon probable cause, supported by oath or affirmation, and particularly describing the place to be searched, and the persons or things to be seized. The Court has interpreted this language to, among other things, prevent judges from issuing warrants that are based on vague or doubtful facts.

Search warrants are often employed early in an investigation, sometimes before the identity of any likely criminal is known. Indeed, these warrants may be used to search the property of purportedly blameless persons. On the other hand, where the material seized falls within First Amendment protection, a search warrant may not be sufficient to protect a citizen's Fourth Amendment right. For example, the Court has held that the particularity requirement must be more strictly adhered to when a First Amendment right is involved.

The Supreme Court has held that the Fourth Amendment's second clause contains four requirements: (1) probable cause, (2) supported by oath or affirmation, particularly describing (3) the place to be searched; and (4) the things to be seized. Probable cause is examined in Chapter 2.

THE FOURTH AMENDMENT'S SECOND CLAUSE—PARTICULARITY

A search conducted pursuant to a warrant that fails to conform to the particularity requirement of the Fourth Amendment is unconstitutional. Moreover, the Court has claimed that the particularity requirement prevents general searches and assures individuals that an officer executing a search warrant has the lawful power to search, and that there are limits on that power.

A warrant that satisfies *some* but not *all* of the four requirements is facially deficient and therefore unconstitutional. However, a court may determine that a facially invalid warrant is constitutional where the warrant's specific language makes reference to a supporting application or affidavit. So, if the warrant uses appropriate words of incorporation, and if the supporting document accompanying the warrant supports probable cause, the warrant is constitutional.

THE FOURTH AMENDMENT'S SECOND CLAUSE—OATH OR AFFIRMATION

Warrants to search or seize must set forth probable cause supported by oath or affirmation. The Supreme Court has emphatically determined that this sworn statement of probable cause must be independently sufficient to inform the judge that probable cause exists.

One of the issues resolved in *Whiteley v. Warden* was whether the citizen's arrest was constitutional where the arrest was based on an arrest warrant whose sole support was the sheriff's *sworn*, but conclusory statements. The *Whiteley* Court easily concluded that the *sworn* complaint standing alone was insufficient to support the independent judgment of a disinterested magistrate. Moreover, the Court rejected the dissent's contention that there was other information in the record that could supplement the sheriff's sworn complaint and thereby support a sufficient basis for probable cause. Although *Whiteley*'s precedential value regarding the application of the exclusionary rule has been questioned, and although it is apparently not controlling precedent involving the truth of an affidavit for a warrant, the Court has consistently confirmed that it clearly retains relevance in determining whether police officers have violated the Fourth Amendment.

THE FOURTH AMENDMENT'S SECOND CLAUSE—PARTICULARLY DESCRIBING...

The Supreme Court has consistently maintained that the constitutional requirement that a warrant must particularly describe the things to be seized is to be accorded the most scrupulous exactitude when the things are books, and the basis for their seizure are the ideas that they contain. First Amendment cases are treated differently from other search and seizure cases. When First Amendment rights are not involved, the particularity requirement is more flexible. The Court has recognized a police officer's good faith reliance on a search warrant authorizing the search of a suspect's third-floor apartment even when the officer did not learn that the third floor contained two apartments, one not belonging to the suspect, until the police executed the search warrant.

NEUTRAL AND DETACHED MAGISTRATE

Unlike the Fourth Amendment warrant requirements of probable cause, oath or affirmation, and particularity as to search of a place and the seizure of things, there is no specific language about a neutral and detached magistrate. Instead the Supreme Court has adopted this requirement based on a number of precedents. In essence this requirement provides that inferences necessary for determining whether a warrant is valid should be drawn by a neutral and detached magistrate instead of being judged by the officer engaged in the often competitive enterprise of ferreting out crime. Consequently, warrants are unconstitutional under the Fourth Amendment when issued by a state agent who is not neutral or detached. A state agent is not rendered neutral and detached merely by having authority to issue warrants. Also, the issuing magistrate need not be a lawyer or a judge. As a consequence, a municipal court clerk can be a neutral and detached magistrate, but if the clerk is paid only if arrest warrants are issued, then the clerk is neither neutral nor detached.

Knock and Announce—The Manner of Entry

Generally, a search or seizure conducted without a warrant is presumptively unreasonable. However, even where the police possess a warrant to search and seize in a citizen's home the search or seizure may be unreasonable where the manner of entry was unreasonable. The reasonableness of a search of a dwelling may depend in part on whether law enforcement officers announced their presence and authority prior to entering. Even under these circumstances, the Court has acknowledged that there is nothing specific about the formalities or the manner of conducting a search or seizure. Moreover, the Court has eschewed the use of categories or protocols when determining the reasonable execution of a warrant.

Instead of categories, the Court examines the totality of the circumstances in each case in order to determine whether the manner of entry was reasonable. As a result, the Court has identified factual considerations of unusual, albeit not dispositive, significance. For example, generally, the Court requires the police to announce their intent to enter before entering closed premises. However, the police may make an unannounced entry where they have reason to believe that evidence would likely be destroyed if advance notice were given.

To justify a no-knock entry the police must possess a reasonable belief or suspicion that the knock will cause the citizen to harm the policeman or destroy evidence. When determining whether the police had reasonable suspicion that announcing their presence might be dangerous to themselves or others, the Court has decided that the existence of reasonable suspicion does not depend on whether the police must destroy property to enter the closed premises. The Court has noted that excessive or unnecessary destruction of property in the course of a search may violate the Fourth Amendment, even though the entry itself is otherwise lawful and the fruits of the search not subject to suppression.

Although the police may persuade a judge prior to entry that reasonable suspicion exists to justify a no-knock entry, sometimes an exigency may arise after the police have knocked and announced. After they have done so, the issue becomes: How long must they wait before entering the premises? According to the Court, the facts known to the police are used in judging a reasonable waiting time. Then, a judge must examine the disposal time of the particular evidence involved in order to determine whether the officer's claim of exigent need was reasonable. Where evidence is not readily destructible, police should wait longer before entering after knocking and announcing. Obviously, each case must be determined on its own facts.

So, even where the police enter closed premises with a warrant, the reasonableness inquiry under the Fourth Amendment has not ended. Next, a trial judge may be required to determine if the manner of entry was reasonable. Such a determination may depend on whether the police (1) knocked and announced; (2) waited for a reasonable period of time (after knocking and announcing), or recognized an exigency after knocking and announcing; or (3) destroyed property before, after, or without knocking and announcing. At one time, the presumption was that where the manner of entry was unreasonable (failing to knock and announce) then any fruits discovered upon entry would be excluded pursuant to the exclusionary rule. This presumption is no longer valid when the police enter pursuant to a search warrant.

The Remedy for Violating the Knock-and-Announce Requirement

In *Wong Sun v. United States*, the Court held, among other things, that where incriminating evidence against the accused is discovered by the unconstitutional actions of the police, in order to determine whether to exclude the incriminating evidence, a court must decide

> Whether granting establishment of the primary illegality, the evidence to which instant objection is made has been come at by exploitation of that illegality or instead by means sufficiently distinguishable to be purged of the primary taint.

Pursuant to *Wong Sun*, the *taint* of the unconstitutional police conduct may be removed or purged through a process called *attenuation*. If the *taint* is removed, the incriminating evidence may be admitted into evidence against the accused. *Wong Sun* defined *attenuation* as follows:

> Attenuation can occur, of course, when the casual connection is remote… [or] the interest protected by the constitutional guarantee that has been violated would not be served by suppression of the evidence obtained.

In *Hudson v. Michigan*, the Court declared that exclusion may not be premised on the mere fact that a constitutional violation was a but-for cause of obtaining evidence. That is, the but-for causality is only a necessary, not a sufficient condition for suppression.

According to the *Hudson* Court the connection between the illegal police conduct and the discovered evidence becomes attenuated or dissipated (1) when the causal link is remote, or (2) even when there is a direct causal connection, but the interest protected by the constitutional guarantee that has been violated would not be served by suppressing the discovered evidence.

After *Hudson v. Michigan*, evidence identified in and discovered pursuant to a search warrant will not be excluded at trial even if the police entered by failing to knock and announce. The *Hudson* Court concedes, however, that a failure to knock and announce is a necessary, not a sufficient, condition for suppression. How then, does or should such an entry affect plain-view seizures or other incriminating evidence discovered during a lawful search?

Plain View—Executing a Warrant, Etc.

The Supreme Court has attempted to describe the common features of the *plain-view* (seizing evidence without a warrant) doctrine exception to the warrant requirement:

> What the plainview cases have in common is that the police officer in each of them had a prior justification for intrusion in the course of which he came *inadvertently* across a piece of evidence incriminating to the accused.

After *Horton v. California*, plain view no longer requires an inadvertence component.

The police are required to have prior justification for their presence in order for the plain-view doctrine to apply. Prior justification has included (1) searching for *other* objects pursuant to a warrant, (2) hot pursuit, (3) search incident to a lawful arrest, and (4) presence of an officer for some other legitimate reason unconnected with the search directed against the accused, which permits the warrantless seizure. However, the evidence must be immediately apparent to the seizing officer.

Hudson v. Michigan concedes that a policeman's failure to knock and announce when executing a warrant violates precedent and therefore may result in the officer entering the premises in an unconstitutional manner. However, if the exclusionary rule does not apply to evidence identified in the warrant, it would not according to this reasoning exclude evidence found in plain view or in places where the warrant allowed the police to search.

HYPOTHETICAL

Police Chief Marck Jackson (hereafter "Chief Jackson") of the Fayetteberg Police Department found the following anonymous letter under his office door around 7:30 am on May 29, 2004:

> I am an employee at Wal-Market Super Center on 12th Street in Fayetteberg. You should know that several people on the Wal-Market management staff at this store are selling powdered cocaine to kids at Fayetteberg High School and Romney Jr. High. Two kids at Romney Jr. High died from overdosing on this toxic dope. The street name of this cocaine is "Triple H."
>
> By the way, some of these Wal-Market managers are quite well-known in the community. Two of them are named "Bob." You know them well! They brag on how they've made so much money selling drugs and how they can hide it through their regular jobs. They sell the cocaine from the employee restrooms at the 12th Street store. They also use the employee lockers to store (and sometimes sell from) the drugs. The drugs are sometimes stored in their cars. Sometimes they sold drugs from a house on Dayton Place. You can usually tell drugs are being sold when cars stop at the gate and people go in without a paper sack but come out with a paper sack.

Chief Jackson conducted a search of police files to determine if any students from Romney Jr. High had recently died of toxic drugs. After a two-hour search he found records of three recent deaths by toxic drugs. Two of these deaths were of seventh graders at Canal Jr. High. The other death was of an eighth grader at Romney Jr. High. Chief Jackson also had several tips from reliable informants that "Bob" Sample sold drugs in the neighborhood.

After this search, Chief Jackson called the Wal-Market Home Office in Collierville. Chief Jackson identified himself and asked the appropriate personnel to locate the full name and address of the manager, "Jim Bob," at the 12th Street Super Center. After a ninety-minute search, the Home Office confirmed that there were two employee-managers at that store named "Bob." "Jim Bob" Sample was not only in his seventh year as a manager, but he was also a popular country-western singer in the Ozarks, and James Robert ("Bob") Powell was a two-year veteran and a popular thespian in a local theater troupe. "Bob" Powell, however, was on duty at a Wal-Market in China. So, Chief Jackson dispatched six officers to "Bob" Sample's home at 2342 Dayton Place in Fayetteberg.

Chief Jackson's team of six officers was led by Officer Frank Pendleton. Officer Pendleton was a ten-year veteran. When Pendleton and his team arrived at 2342 Dayton Place they discovered that they could not observe, from ground level, a greenhouse located in the backyard of the property nor could they see any other aspects of the house. They were not able to see any exterior details of the house or the greenhouse because the property was totally enclosed by a ten-foot-high oak paneled fence that had several "DO NOT ENTER" signs written in red ink posted at each corner. Despite these obstacles Officer Pendleton persevered. Indeed, he was able to view (and record the license plate number) of all the people who drove up to, entered, and exited the metal-and-oak door built into the ten-foot oak fence. His written report (and the subsequent affidavit) noted that this door had an obvious peephole in its center. During a two-hour observation period Officer Pendleton and his team of officers observed and noted at least seven cars drive up to the metal-and-oak door. Although each car contained several occupants, only the occupant in the front passenger seat emerged and entered through the door.

All the visitors were young men between twenty and thirty years of age. Half of the *visitors* were either Hispanic or African-American. The rest were white. Each *visitor* was observed (and noted) knocking twice on the door while he cautiously looked up and down the street. None of the visitors carried anything in their hands. Immediately the door would open and the *visitor* would quickly enter. As the visitor began to enter the door would begin to close. Consequently, after the *visitor* entered the door would instantly close behind him. After a minute or less the door would reopen and the *visitor* hurriedly emerged carrying a small brown paper bag. Then the *visitor* would leap into the waiting car and quickly drive away. One of the seven visitors was recognized by Officer Pendleton as a known drug user: "Snow Ball" (a white male about six feet tall).

Officer Pendleton and his team had assumed positions in two squad cars approximately one hundred yards from 2342 Dayton Place. After getting out of the car and moving to the partially see-through gate door, Officer Pendleton could see through a small crack in the walls at the first-floor level. Here he saw one marijuana plant in "Bob" Sample's first-floor hall closet.

Armed with (1) the anonymous letter, (2) the "findings" of Chief Jackson's investigation, (3) the surveillance observations regarding the seven *visitors*, and (4) his close observation through a crack in the wall, Officer Pendleton secured a search warrant to search Sample's residence and greenhouse area. Officer Pendleton broke down the door as he announced in a loud voice, "Police, we're here to conduct a search of the premises." Officer Pendleton was accompanied by eight officers. Simultaneously twelve other officers entered the back door to the Sample house and the greenhouse nearby. Before Sample could react to Pendleton's announcement, Officer Pendleton and his team had entered the house. Five pounds of cocaine were lying openly on Sample's coffee table. Sample and his lady friend (Chancé James) were arrested. Both were searched. A pound of cocaine was found attached to Sample's back. James had thirty freshly rolled "blunts" (marijuana wrapped) in her purse. One marijuana plant was found in the first-floor closet, and sixty bags of cocaine were found in the nearby greenhouse.

Bob Sample and James have hired lawyers. At that arraignment Sample and James will request that all of the evidence be suppressed. You are an associate prosecutor. Please provide your senior prosecutor with a memorandum of law (1) analyzing the key legal precedents that the defendants will likely use to support their motions, (2) isolating the most persuasive arguments distilled from those precedents, and (3) predicting how the court is likely to rule on these competing arguments.

LIST OF READINGS

1. The Fourth Amendment to the United States Constitution.
2. Federal Rules of Evidence Rule 401. Definition of Relevant Evidence.
3. Federal Rules of Evidence Rule 402. Relevant Evidence Generally Admissible; Irrelevant Evidence Inadmissible.
4. *Coolidge v. New Hampshire*, 403 U.S. 443 (1971).
5. *Whiteley v. Warden*, 401 U.S. 560 1971), but see *Arizona v. Evans*, 514 U.S. 1, 14 (1995) (rejecting parts of *Whiteley*).
6. *Steele v. United States*, 267 U.S. 498 (1925).
7. *Groh v. Ramirez*, 540 U.S. 551 (2004).
8. *Stanford v. Texas*, 379 U.S. 476 (1964).
9. *Zurcher v. Stanford Daily*, 436 U.S. 547 (1978).
10. *Boyd v. United States*, 116 U.S. 616 (1886).
11. *Winston v. Lee*, 470 U.S. 753 (1985).
12. *A Quantity of Books v. Kansas*, 378 U.S. 205 (1964).
13. *Marcus v. Search Warrant*, 367 U.S. 717 (1961).
14. *Lee Art Theatre, Inc. v. Virginia*, 392 U.S. 636 (1968) (*per curiam*).
15. *Arizona v. Evans*, 514 U.S. 1 (1995).
16. *Johnson v. United States*, 333 U.S. 10 (1948).
17. *Katz v. United States*, 389 U.S. 347 (1967).
18. *Wilson v. Arkansas*, 514 U.S. 927 (1995).
19. *United States v. Banks*, 540 U.S. 31 (2003).
20. *Richards v. Wisconsin*, 520 U.S. 385 (1997).
21. *Ker v. California*, 374 U.S. 23 (1963).
22. *United States v. Ramirez*, 523 U.S. 65 (1998).
23. *Wong Sun v. United States*, 371 U.S. 471 (1963).
24. *Hudson v. Michigan*, 547 U.S. 586 (2006).
25. *Horton v. California*, 496 U.S. 128 (1990).
26. *Arizona v. Hicks*, 480 U.S. 321 (1987).

SAMPLE ESSAY

To: Senior Prosecutor
From: Associate Prosecutor
Re: Suppression Hearing—[*State v. Sample and Jones*]
Defendant's motions to exclude cocaine and marijuana plants seized pursuant to a warrant and a search incident to an arrest
Date:

In anticipation of the forthcoming motions-in-limine by the defendants as described above, I have prepared the following memorandum of law for your consideration. As you will discover this memorandum attempts to (1) identify the key legal precedents that the defendants will use to support their likely motions under the facts set out below, (2) isolate the most persuasive arguments distilled from these precedents that they are likely to assert (and our counterarguments to them), and (3) predict how the court is likely to rule on these competing arguments.

Although the police had a warrant when they entered the defendants' premises, the defendants will argue the police entered *unreasonably* because they failed to knock and announce. Because the entry was unreasonable, they will argue that the fruits of the subsequent searches and seizures are tainted and thereby subject to exclusion as fruits of the poisonous tree. We should readily concede that the police did not knock and announce, because the current knock-and-announce law supports admissibility of all the seized evidence.

At first blush, the defendant's use of *Wilson v. Arkansas* may appear helpful to them. However, this is a false appearance because the Supreme Court's most recent decision on the knock-and-announce doctrine, *Hudson v. Michigan*, firmly supports our position of admitting all the discovered evidence. According to the *Hudson* Court the connection between the illegal police conduct (failing to knock and announce), and the discovered fruits (evidence incriminating the accused), becomes attenuated or broken when, as under our facts, the interest (privacy) protected by the applicable constitutional doctrine (the Fourth Amendment) that has been violated would not be served by suppressing the discovered evidence.

Unlike the citizen who has been the victim of a warrantless search, the victim of a knock-and-announce violation has different issues to be considered. The knock-and- announce requirement (1) protects the citizen's life and limb, because an unannounced entry may lend to violence; (2) provides the citizen with a peaceful opportunity to comply with the government's demand; and (3) protects elements of the citizen's privacy and dignity that may be destroyed by the police's sudden unannounced entry. As the entry by the police under our facts does not implicate any of those interests protected by the knock-and-announce doctrine, the exclusionary rule is not applicable.

The defendants may, however, argue the position taken by the dissent in *Hudson v. Michigan* that

> [s]eparating the "manner of entry" from the related search slices the violation too finely… we have described a failure to comply with the knock-and-announce rule, not as an independently unlawful event, but as a factor that renders the search "constitutionally defective."

547 U.S. at 615 (Bryer, J., et al., dissenting). That is, they will argue compliance with the knock-and-announce requirement is one of the factors to be considered in assessing the reasonableness of a search or seizure. Yes, we will reply, that is true when the issue is a warrantless entry, because different interests are at stake in the warrantless entry context: shielding potential evidence from government eyes. However, the police had a warrant in our case.

Perhaps the defendants will seek to argue that the police department, and the courts, has engaged in a widespread pattern of violations against persons who lack the means or voice to mount an effective protest. Although the concurrence in *Hudson* raises this possibility, I believe this theory is too vague or ill described to earn the confidence of the court. Still, it may be wise to check the police history of such searches to determine if there is any evidence of such a pattern.

TOOLS FOR SELF-CRITICISM

The second paragraph of the essay provides that the defendants will argue that the police entered the accused's home unreasonably in violation of the Fourth

Amendment by failing to knock and announce their presence. The police concede that they did not knock and announce. As a result, the defendants contend that under such circumstances the Supreme Court has held that the common law knock-and-announce principle forms a part of the reasonableness inquiry under the Fourth Amendment. However, the defendant's argument is about how the manner of entry is subject to a reasonableness inquiry. Again, the state concedes that an illegal manner of entry occurred. Because this illegal manner of entry is an unreasonable one under the Fourth Amendment, the defendants' presume that the fruits discovered subsequent to this entry are subject to exclusion under the exclusionary rule. According to the Supreme Court fruits derived by, directly or indirectly, exploiting that primary illegality are subject to exclusion under the exclusionary rule.

The essay does not emphasize that the most cogent argument supporting exclusion is based on *Wong Sun* (the seminal "fruit of the poisonous tree" opinion)

> We need not hold that all evidence is "fruit of the poisonous tree" simply because it would not have come to light but for the illegal actions of the police. Rather, the more apt question in such a case is "whether, granting establishment of the primary illegality, the evidence to which instant objection is made has been come at by exploitation of that illegality or instead by means sufficiently distinguishable to be purged of the primary taint."

So, evidence derived from either a direct or an indirect invasion of a citizen's con stitutional right was not admissible against the accused at trial. Subsequent to *Wong Sun* the Supreme Court consistently held that the sanction of exclusion applied to any fruits of a constitutional violation whether the fruits were tangible, physical items, or words overheard during the unlawful police activity, *United States v. Giordano*, 416 U.S. 505 (1974), or confessions or statements obtained during an illegal arrest or detention, *Dunaway v. New York*, 442 U.S. 200 (1979); *Brown v. Illinois*, 422 U.S. 590 (1975).

On the other hand, the essay did discuss how the sanction of exclusion was not appropriate. The challenged evidence is in no sense the product of illegal governmental activity, or the evidence subject to the defendant's objection was come at by means sufficiently distinguishable to be purged of the primary taint: attenuation. However, the essay failed to elaborate that the Court has consistently admitted evi dence, despite unlawful police conduct, where the official evidence was remote from or independent of that unlawful police conduct. And, despite a primary illegality the Court has held exclusion inappropriate where the evidence objected to would have been inevitably discovered.

Prior to *Hudson v. Michigan* the Supreme Court usually determined that the exclusionary rule was appropriate to exclude evidence causally linked to or tainted by unlawful police conduct. However, the Court has generally held that the exclusionary rule is not appropriate to exclude evidence that was attenuated from that primary illegality because it was either remote from or independent of that unlawful conduct. In *Hudson v. Michigan*, the Court has developed a new method for determining attenuation or the inapplicability of the exclusionary rule.

The essay failed to examine the *Hudson* Court's general posture when examining the exclusionary rule: "Suppression of evidence, however, has always been our last resort, not our first impulse. The exclusionary rule generates 'substantial social costs.' " The *Hudson* Court acknowledged that it has not always spoken so guardedly.

In any event, the presumption that a Fourth Amendment unreasonable entry causally linked to fruits (evidence incriminating to the owner discovered upon entry) renders such fruits subject to exclusion under the exclusionary rule is no longer valid. Apparently the *Hudson* Court has concluded that the exclusionary rule is applicable to most warrantless searches, but that rule is inapplicable to *some* or all with-warrant searches. Unlike the exclusion of the fruits discovered after a warrantless search and seizure, the Court has opined that the exclusionary rule is inappropriate for vindicating the interests protected by the knock-and-announce requirement.

> What the knock-and-announce rule has never protected, however, is one's interest in preventing the government from seeing or taking evidence described in a warrant. Since the interests that were violated in this case have nothing to do with the seizure of the evidence, the exclusionary rule is inapplicable.

547 U.S. at 594. Besides, saying that "it's so, because we say it's so!" the Court offers little, if any, justification for its distinction between the applicability of the exclusionary rule to warrantless searches and seizures, and its inapplicability to warrant-based searches. Thus, the emphasis in the essay, though understandable from a prosecutor's perspective, appears misplaced. The *Hudson* Court, unlike the essay, justified its conclusion that the exclusionary rule was inapplicable more on the basis that (1) the exclusionary rule's deterrence effects are outweighed by its substantial social costs, (2) there are other deterrent remedies equally as effective as exclusion; and (3) a trio of precedents supported the Court's conclusion that the exclusionary rule did not apply to items identified in a search warrant even if the manner of entry was unreasonable. Suffice it to say none of these other reasons for the *Hudson* Court's decision supports the defendants' arguments for exclusion.

CONSENT SEARCHES 4

OPENING REMARKS

Generally

The Fourth Amendment to the United States Constitution prohibits unreasonable searches and seizures. A search without a warrant by government agents is presumptively unreasonable. Even so, under certain circumstances, the Supreme Court has recognized that a warrantless search does not offend the Fourth Amendment. A search conducted pursuant to valid consent is an exception to both the probable cause and the warrant requirements of the Fourth Amendment. The Court has developed several lines of consent-search jurisprudence: (1) citizen-defendant consent searches, (2) third-party consent—citizen with actual authority, and (3) third-party consent—citizen with apparent authority. Our hypothetical is based on the *apparent* authority variety.

Defining consent is a critical step in order to determine the applicable line of jurisprudence. Generally, the police search of property without a warrant or without probable cause is constitutional if it was made pursuant to voluntary consent. The Supreme Court has held that the question of whether consent was voluntary or the product of duress or coercion is a question for the courts. In any event, the Court has concluded that voluntariness is to be determined from all the circumstances. The Court has also held that the confessor's knowledge of a right to refuse consent may be a factor in the totality of the circumstances, but not a dispositive one.

Involuntary consent occurs when the circumstances created by the police cause the target (confessing party) of the search surprise confusion or fright—so much so that the citizen's will to say no is overcome. Similarly, consent has been invalidated where it was the product of threats. Courts have considered many factors in the totality of the circumstances.

Citizen Yields to a Policeman's Claim of Authority to Search Pursuant to a Warrant—Acquiescence

The Court has held that there is no voluntary consent when a citizen complies with a policeman's untruthful assertion that he possessed a warrant to conduct a search. Such a concession is not voluntary consent, but unlawful acquiescence. A citizen who acquiesces to a policeman's claim of authority cannot voluntarily consent.

Third-Party Consent—Actual Authority versus Apparent Authority

Where a person other than the target of the search gives consent to the police another type of consent analysis applies: third-party consent. Under the third-party consent exception, the Supreme Court has held that consent may be obtained from someone other than the target of the search. There are two varieties of third-party consent. Each will be briefly examined in turn.

First is the actual authority variety. Under this category of consent, in order for a third party to have authority to give consent, he must (actually) possess common authority over or have other sufficient relationship to the premises or effects sought to be searched. A prosecutor offering to prove third-party consent pursuant to this theory must show that the third-party consenter possessed common authority over the premises, and that possession is valid against the absent non-consenting person with whom that authority is shared. Consequently, the target (non-consenting party) of the search has assumed the risk that the third-party consenter would admit others.

Second is the apparent authority variety. This type of third-party consent does not require either joint access or assumption of risk. The Supreme Court has said that as with other factual determinations bearing upon search and seizure, determination of consent to enter must be judged against an objective standard: Would the facts available to the officer at the moment warrant a man of reasonable caution in the belief' (apparent) that the consenting party had authority over the premises? Hence, if a third party appears to have actual authority and the police reasonably rely on that appearance, the consent is valid. Indeed, the officer's reasonable reliance may be incorrect, but such an error will not invalidate a third-party consent because the Fourth Amendment only requires the government to act reasonably. Under this version of third-party consent the test is reasonableness.

The Non-consenting Occupant Objects

The Supreme Court has held in *United States v. Matlock* that the police may lawfully enter, without a warrant, the house of a non-consenting/absent citizen occupant on the basis of the voluntary consent of his co-occupant who possesses actual authority over the premises. Similarly, the Court has held in *Illinois v. Rodriquez* that the police may lawfully enter, without a warrant, the home of a non-consenting/absent citizen occupant on the basis that the police reasonably believe that the person who gave consent had the authority to do so. However, the Court has recently held in *Georgia v. Randolph* that when the police conduct a warrantless search, authorized by one co-occupant, over the express objection of another (present) co-occupant, that search is unreasonable as to the objecting co-occupant.

In so holding, the *Randolph* Court carefully distinguished and preserved two earlier opinions defining consent searches. The Court reconciled *United States v. Matlock* and *Illinois v. Rodriguez* by first noting that its rule was applicable as long as there is no evidence that the police have removed the potentially objecting occupant from the premises for the sake of avoiding a possible objection to a search. Having stated that precondition; the Court concluded that simple clarity of the complimentary rules required a court to recognize that a co-occupant's consent was controlling in the absence of his roommate. On the other hand, the co-occupant's consent must yield to the express objection of his present non-consenting co-occupant. Moreover, the Court determined that where the police receive the voluntary consent of a co-occupant they need not take affirmative steps to find a potentially objecting co-occupant before acting on the permission they had already received.

The Scope of a Consent Search

Although the Court has stated that the scope of a search is generally defined by its expressed objective, it cited a case that specifically applied to the automobile exception. Nevertheless, the Court has applied this definition to a consent search. According to the Court where a policeman receives a citizen's voluntary consent to search the citizen's car for narcotics, it is objectively reasonable for the police to conclude that the general consent to search the citizen's car included the consent to search containers within the car that might contain drugs (or the object of the search).

HYPOTHETICAL

Police Chief Marck Jackson (hereafter "Chief Jackson") of the Fayetteberg Police Department found the following anonymous letter under his office door around 7:30 am on May 29, 2004:

> I am an employee at Wal-Market Super Center on 12th Street in Fayetteberg. You should know that several people on the Wal-Market management staff at this store are selling powdered cocaine to kids at Fayetteberg High School and Romney Jr. High. Two kids at Romney Jr. High died from overdosing on this toxic dope. The street name of this cocaine is "Triple H."
>
> By the way, some of these Wal-Market managers are quite well-known in the community. Two of them are named "Bob." You know them well! They brag on how they've made so much money selling drugs and how they can hide it through their regular jobs. They sell the cocaine from the employee restrooms at the 12th Street store. They also use the employee lockers to store (and sometimes sell from) the drugs. The drugs are sometimes stored in their cars.

Chief Jackson conducted a search of police files to determine if any students from Romney Jr. High had recently died of toxic drugs. After a two-hour search he found records of three recent deaths by toxic drugs. Two of these deaths were of seventh graders at Canal Jr. High. The other death was of an eighth grader at Romney Jr. High. Chief Jackson also had several tips from reliable informants that "Bob" Sample sold drugs in the neighborhood.

After this search, Chief Jackson called the Wal-Market Home Office in Collierville. Chief Jackson identified himself and asked the appropriate personnel to locate the full name and address of the manager, "Jim Bob," at the 12th Street Super Center. After a ninety-minute search, the Home Office confirmed that there were two employee-managers at that store named "Bob." "Jim Bob" Sample was not only in his seventh year as a manager, but he was also a popular country-western singer in the Ozarks and James Robert ("Bob") Powell was a two-year veteran and a popular thespian in a local theater troupe. "Bob" Powell, however, was on duty at a Wal-Market in China. So, Chief Jackson dispatched six officers to "Bob" Sample's home at 2342 Dayton Place.

When the six officers arrived at 2342 Dayton Place, they saw a woman dressed in overalls with a "leaves are us" emblem on her back (and a similar emblem was on a truck parked at the curb nearby) mowing the grass at that address. She stopped mowing and asked the officers whether they were coming to arrest her paramour, "Bob" Sample. She said (before they could answer), "I told him he was going to get arrested for engaging in illegal activities. But he wouldn't listen to me. Go on inside—the door is unlocked. He's inside asleep in our bedroom."

The officers pushed open the unlocked door and found "Bob" Sample asleep on the sofa. Two pounds of cocaine was found openly displayed on the coffee table. Sample was arrested and charged with felony possession of a controlled substance with intent to distribute. Sample's defense attorney has moved to exclude this marijuana because he claims Sample's Fourth Amendment Rights were violated. As associate to the Deputy Prosecutor, identify two arguments the defense may raise at this suppression hearing and how the state can successfully respond to them. [We have subsequently learned that the young woman mowing the lawn was not "Bob" Sample's paramour; she was lying about living there].

LIST OF READINGS

1. The Fourth Amendment to the United States Constitution.
2. Federal Rules of Evidence Rule 401. Definition of Relevant Evidence
3. Federal Rules of Evidence Rule 402. Relevant Evidence Generally Admissible; Irrelevant Evidence Inadmissible.
4. *Horton v. California*, 496 U.S. 128 (1990).
5. *Katz v. United States*, 389 U.S. 347 (1967).
6. *Carroll v. United States*, 267 U.S. 132 (1925).
7. *Schneckloth v. Bustamonte*, 412 U.S. 218 (1973).
8. *United States v. Matlock*, 415 U.S. 164 (1974).
9. *Illinois v. Rodriguez*, 497 U.S. 177 (1990).
10. *Georgia v. Randolph,* 547 U.S. 103 (2006).
11. 4 Wayne R. LaFave, Search and Seizure § 8.3(g) at 180 (4th ed. 2004).
12. Survey. The Fourth Amendment, Password-Protected Computer Files and Third Party Consent Searches: The Tenth Circuit Broadens the Scope of Warrantless Searches, 85 Den. U. L. Rev. 701 (2008).
13. Daniel Williams, Misplaced Angst: Another Look at Consent Search Jurisprudence, 82 Ind. L.J. 69 (Winter 2007).
14. Note, You Say Yes, But Can I Say No?: The Future of Third-Party Consent Searches after *Georgia v. Randolph*, 73 Brook. L. Rev. 421 (2007);
15. Note: Third Party Consent Searches after *Georgia v. Randolph*: Dueling Approaches to the Dueling Roommates, 87 B.U. L. Rev. 937 (2007).
16. Note: The Fourth Amendment and Antidilution: Confronting the Overlooked Function of the Consent Search Doctrine, 119 Harv. L. Rev. 2187 (2006).

SAMPLE ESSAY

To: Senior Prosecutor
From: Associate Prosecutor
Re: Pretrial Proceedings—Defendant's Motion in Limine—to suppress contraband seized pursuant to a warrantless entry.

Date:

In anticipation of the upcoming motion-in-limine by the defendant described above, I have prepared the following memorandum explaining the issues involved and our possible response to this motion. Essentially the defendant will argue that the police entered his premises without a warrant or other lawful justification and therefore the marijuana found inside should be excluded from his trial. In response, I believe we can show that the police lawfully entered (third-party consent) the premises and then seized the marijuana lying in plain view.

As consent is the Fourth Amendment exception that I recommend we adopt to justify the warrantless police entry to the premises, the applicable case law requires that at a minimum we show that the facts available to the officer at the time of his entry and seizure warranted a reasonable belief that the consenting person appeared to have authority over the premises. Of course, if we fail to successfully show that the police entry was made pursuant to a valid consent, the officer's testimony about the entry and the seized marijuana will be excluded from the defendant's trial. Accordingly, if this evidence is excluded the court will dismiss this charge against the defendant. In any event, my analysis of how we may prevail in this matter is set out in several parts below.

PART A. THE GENERAL RULE OF ADMISSIBILITY

The Federal Rules of Evidence provide that all relevant evidence is admissible except as otherwise provided by the Constitution of the United States. Because the Fourth Amendment to the United States Constitution prohibits unreasonable searches and seizures, any unreasonable search or seizure violates the Fourth Amendment. For example, the Supreme Court has held that a warrantless search of a citizen's property by an agent of the government violates the Fourth Amendment. More important, in order to insure the effectiveness of this Fourth Amendment protection, the Supreme Court has held that evidence seized as a result of the unlawful search could not constitute proof at trial against the victim of the search.

At the pretrial proceedings the judge must consider whether under the facts and law of this case the police lawfully entered the defendant's premises pursuant to valid consent from a third party. If so, then the seizure of the marijuana was constitutional, and the motion should not be granted. An analysis of the law applied to the facts of our case follows.

PART B. THIRD-PARTY CONSENT

At the suppression hearing we should expect the defendant to contend that the Fourth Amendment protects him from unreasonable searches and seizures. Here he will claim that the police violated his Fourth Amendment rights by entering his house without a warrant. The defendant will then argue that the court should exclude the marijuana from the trial because it is the fruit of a warrantless entry. Therefore the admissibility of the marijuana at the defendant's trial will turn on whether the warrantless police entry was lawful.

In this case the police did not have a warrant or probable cause plus an exigency to enter defendant's house. However, neither a warrant nor probable cause plus an exigency is required where the police obtain consent to enter the premises. On our facts the police purportedly received consent from a third person who appeared to have authority over the house. The judge at the suppression hearing must evaluate whether this purported consent satisfies the Supreme Court's requirements for valid third-party consent.

In *Illinois v. Rodriguez,* the United States Supreme Court held that a warrantless entry to search and seize is lawful if the police reasonably, but mistakenly, believe that the person giving consent had sufficient authority over the searched property to give consent.

The Court reached this answer by initially observing that in this case the police were summoned to the home of the mom of an alleged assault victim. The police were met by the alleged victim, who showed signs of a severe beating. The victim told the police she had been assaulted by the defendant earlier that day at an apartment in town. She also told the police that the defendant was presently asleep in that apartment. She agreed to travel to that apartment with the police in order to unlock the door with her key so that the officers could enter and arrest him. Several times during this conversation (with the police) she referred to the apartment as "our" apartment, and she said she had clothes and furniture there.

Neither before nor while driving the victim to the apartment did the police obtain an arrest warrant for the defendant, nor did they seek a search warrant for the apartment. At the apartment, the victim unlocked the door with "her key" and gave the officers permission to enter. The police moved through the door into the living room, where they observed in plain view drug paraphernalia and containers filled with white powder that they believed (correctly, as later analysis showed) to be cocaine. The police proceeded to the bedroom, where they found the defendant asleep. They found additional containers of cocaine in the bedroom. The police arrested the defendant and seized the cocaine and related drug paraphernalia.

The defendant was charged with possession of a controlled substance with intent to deliver. He moved to suppress all the evidence seized at the time of his arrest, claiming that the victim had vacated the apartment several weeks earlier and had no authority to consent to the entry.

Although the Court concluded that the victim lacked actual authority to consent to the police entry because she no longer lived in the apartment, the Court determined that

> What is assured by the Fourth Amendment itself, however, is not that no government search of his house will occur unless he consents; but that no such search will occur that is unreasonable.

So, according to the Court there are "various elements... that can make a search of a person's house 'reasonable'... one of which is the consent of the person or his cotenant," or in another situation where the police officers enter a citizen's house without a warrant because they reasonably (though erroneously) believe that the consenting person is a resident of the premises.

Pursuant to this holding, whenever a trial judge has to decide whether the officer's belief was reasonable, the judge is required to answer this question: Would the facts available to the officers at the moment warrant a man of reasonable caution in the belief that the consenting party had authority over the premises?

Curiously, the Court appears to add another layer to its holding by opining about what its holding does not suggest. In any event, when determining the reasonableness of an officer's belief, the Court instructs a trial court not to always accept a consenter's invitation to enter the premises. Indeed, the Court warns the trial judge that

> Even when the invitation is accompanied by an explicit assertion that the person lives there, the surrounding circumstances could conceivably be such that a reasonable person would doubt its truth and not act upon it without further inquiry.

Hence, on occasion the *surrounding* circumstances may require a reasonable police officer to make further inquiry of a third party about his purported consent.

PART C. THIRD PARTY CONSENT APPLIED TO OUR HYPOTHETICAL

As explained above, we should argue that the warrantless entry by the police was lawful because it was based on a third party's consent. The Supreme Court has held that a third party's consent is lawful if (1) the consenting third party had actual authority over the premises, or (2) the police reasonably (though mistakenly) believed that the consenting third party had actual authority. Our facts limit us to the reasonably believed variety.

The Court has articulated two points of analysis that are applicable to the reasonably believed variety of consent. First, what would the facts communicate to a reasonable police officer at the moment "consent" was purportedly given? Second, even if the third party invites the police to enter the premises, could the "surrounding circumstances" conceivably be such that a reasonable person would doubt the truth of the third party's authority to give consent and not act upon it without further inquiry? Although our hypothetical will be examined by using both approaches, the "*reasonably believed*" variety will ultimately determine this case. At the outset the "*reasonably believed*" approach raises issues about not only what an officer would "*reasonably*" believe upon hearing the purported consent, but what "surrounding circumstances" could "conceivably" compel a reasonable officer to doubt the truth of the third party's authority to give consent and not act upon it without inquiry.

The Supreme Court held that the Constitution is not violated when officers enter premises without a warrant because they reasonably (though erroneously) believe at the time of entry that the third-party consenter possessed the authority to consent. The Court implied that the officer's reliance was reasonable because the third-party consenter (1) referred (several times) to the apartment as "our" apartment, (2) said she had clothes and furniture in the apartment, and (3) unlocked the apartment door with "her key" (in order to allow the police to enter).

Likewise, the Court implied that these factors supporting the officer's reasonable reliance on the third-party's consent *did not* indicate "surrounding circumstances" that could conceivably cause a policeman to doubt the truth of the third party's authority to give consent. Nor would these same factors, according to the Court, require a police officer to make further inquiry of the third-party consenter *before* entering the premises. Although it does not expressly state as much, it is apparent from the Court's language that a trial court may determine the lawfulness of a warrantless entry based on a third party's consent by examining both the facts supporting an officer's reasonable reliance and the "*surrounding circumstances*" that could have conceivably caused the officer to doubt the truth of the third party's consent. Apparently both inquiries are satisfied in the leading case.

Even if a police officer reasonably relies on certain statements or acts by the third-party consenter the presence of "*surrounding circumstances*" may compel the officer to doubt the truth of the authority of the third party to give consent in our case. In our case, the facts supporting a claim of the officer's reasonable reliance include the third party's (1) invitation to the police to enter the premises, (2) assertion that the defendant is her paramour, (3) claim that the defendant was presently in the house, and (4) disclosure that the door to the house was unlocked. Except for using "her key" to unlock the apartment door the third-party consenter in the leading case did not say or do anything significantly different from the third-party consenter in our hypothetical. Accordingly, the police officer in our hypothetical reasonably relied on the third-party consenter.

Unfortunately, this conclusion would not complete the analysis.
One of the facts that the state uses to support its argument that the officer established a reasonable reliance on the third-party's consent is the third-party's "*invitation*" to enter the premises. The leading opinion warns, however, that

> Even when the invitation is accompanied by an explicit assertion that the person lives there, the surrounding circumstances could conceivably be such that a reasonable person would doubt its truth....

The defendant may, as a consequence, trump our showing of reasonable reliance with "*surrounding circumstances.*" Did the "*surrounding circumstances*" in our hypothetical compel the officer to doubt the truthfulness of the purported third-party consenter?

Here, the third party was dressed as a commercial contractor. She was performing her work on the defendant's property. Her verbal assertions and her work in his yard linked her to the defendant's house. In the leading case the third party was not at, in, or on the property when she initially gave consent. However, the third party in the leading case actually used her key to admit the officers. There is no comparable physical showing in our facts. Our third party did reveal that she knew the defendant's door was unlocked and she was working in his yard. Such a showing should satisfy the requirements of the leading case. The problem with this line of analysis is that the leading case did not specifically define or otherwise describe objective reasonable belief.

One of the seminal cases (*Rodriquez*) on third-party consent did not reach the question of whether the officers had an objective reasonable (though mistaken) belief that the person granting access (third-party consenter) to the premises had actual authority over the premises. The case merely determined that the lower court had erroneously ruled that as a matter of law "*reasonable* belief could not validate *entry*." As a consequence, lower courts have had to specifically determine the nature of a policeman's objective reasonable belief.

Underscoring what an officer is required to do when confronted with ambiguous facts, one noted commentator has written:

> sometimes the facts known by the police cry out for further inquiry, and when this is the case it is not reasonable for the police to proceed on the theory that ignorance is bliss.

For example, even if she was accompanied by young children, a third party's mere presence on the premises to be searched is not sufficient to establish that a man of reasonable caution would believe that she had "*mutual use of the property by virtue of joint access, or... control for most purposes....*" According to this reasoning a police officer who arrives at the premises without any information about the third party's relationship to those premises confronts an ambiguous situation.

> When an officer knocks on the door of an apartment at three o'clock in the afternoon, the person who answers the knock could be a repairman, a visitor, or a neighbor watering the plants or feeding the pets.

Although police officers who face ambiguous situations are required (by some courts) to make further inquiry of the purported third-party consenter, other courts have adopted a more liberal approach. That is, some courts have allowed the police to form their impressions (*objectively reasonable reliance*) from the context of the totality of the circumstances. For example, one court held that the police acted reasonably in letting the defendant's sister-in-law admit them to his house, even though she had no key and she had to crawl through a window. In this instance, the court opined that the police were entitled to rely on the sister-in-law's statement that she lived at the house and that she had left her bedroom window unlocked. The court added that the sister-in-law's statement was corroborated when she was able to open that window.

Accordingly, we should argue that the judge in our case adopt the more liberal approach for determining a police officer's objective reasonableness from the context of the totality of the circumstances. Under this approach our officers would be considered objectively reasonable in the context of all the facts. Whether implied from the language of the seminal opinion on third-party consent or whether based on the more liberal approach of some federal courts, the police in our case did not violate the defendant's Fourth Amendment rights.

TOOLS FOR SELF-CRITICISM

The Question Presented and the Answer Offered Based on Applicable Legal Standards

The first paragraph of the essay provides that the state prosecutor will be required to justify the actions of police officers who entered the defendant's premises without either a warrant or probable cause and an exigency. As a result of this *warrantless entry* the police seized contraband lying in *plain view*. In part, defendant's motion asserts that the Fourth Amendment prohibits unreasonable searches and seizures. Defendant will argue that this search and seizure is presumptively unreasonable because the police entered the premises without a warrant, and that therefore the contraband seized from his premises is the inadmissible "*fruit*" (of the "*poisonous tree*") of that warrantless entry.

Although the Fourth Amendment prohibits unreasonable searches and seizures, the state will argue that the warrantless entry and resulting seizure in this case were reasonable because the police received permission to enter the premises from a person they reasonably believed had the authority to admit them.

The facts and goals at the suppression hearing are relatively clear. The law of third-party consent is less so. Paragraph two is an inadequate summary of applicable third-party consent jurisprudence. First, it is inadequate because the two types of third-party consent approved by the Supreme Court are not explained. Second, the seminal opinion distinguishing the two types of third-party consent fails to adequately explain the adopted *standard* (apparent authority) for our analysis. Nevertheless a few *barebone* introductory notes appear necessary to provide the reader (senior prosecutor) with a preview of the essential issue(s) the trial court must decide. Moreover, it is helpful for the senior prosecutor to initially understand the consequences of the state's failure to justify the warrantless entry by the police.

A. The first paragraph of Part A ("the General Rule of Admissibility" Section) adequately explains that even relevant evidence is not admissible (at trial) if it was obtained in an unlawful way. And paragraph two of this section merely announces the upcoming explanation of the applicable law.

B. Part B attempts to explain the genesis of the United States Supreme Court's third-party consent jurisprudence and its applicability to the facts of our hypothetical. Although *Illinois v. Rodriguez* is the most appropriate precedent for our facts, this seminal opinion failed to define or otherwise describe its reasonable belief concept. Indeed, the Court remanded the case to the Illinois Appellate Court in order for that court to determine whether the officers "*reasonably believed*" that the purported third-party consenter had the authority to consent.

   Because *Rodriguez* did not specifically define reasonable belief, the initial discussion (in our essay) of the principles from that opinion concerns what is *implied* about reasonable belief. At first blush, this appears to be the weakest aspect of the state's analysis. However, the follow-up analysis, which is based on interpretations of reasonable belief by lower federal courts, corroborates the conclusions reached under the *implied* analysis. Still, lower federal courts have not uniformly interpreted reasonable belief. So, as there is no uniform standard for reasonable belief, a court may require (under an alternative to our "liberal" approach) officers to show that they made "further *inquiry*" before the judge determines that they reasonably believed that the third-party consenter had actual authority to consent.

C. The essay fails to emphasize or otherwise effectively discuss the factual support for the reasonable belief of the police in the seminal case as contrasted to the facts available to the police in our hypothetical. For more on this issue see Part 6 Variations on a Theme—*infra*.

D. The essay also failed to discuss or comment on the *subsequent* discovery that the purported consenter was not the defendant-Sample's paramour. This discussion was not necessary because the test from the seminal Supreme Court opinion requires the trial court to only consider the facts available to the police at the moment of the purported consent. Consequently, *any* revelation or disclosure made by or to the police *after* the moment *of* consent is not relevant under the Court's reasonable belief test.

VARIATIONS ON A THEME

The central theme of the hypothetical concerns the legality of the warrantless entry by the police. But for this warrantless entry the police would not have found the cocaine in the defendant's home. The discovery of this contraband led to the charges against this citizen-defendant. In order to successfully defend himself against this charge, the citizen must convince a judge that the police entry and seizure violated the Fourth Amendment.

The United States Supreme Court has held that the Fourth Amendment prohibits the police from entering a citizen's home without a warrant. However, the Court has recognized several exceptions to this *general* prohibition. For example, the police may make a lawful warrantless entry pursuant to probable cause and an exigency, or the consent of a citizen, or the consent of a third party who has either actual or apparent authority.

No Anonymous Letter

In our hypothetical the police chief dispatched officers to the citizen's home because the police chief (1) read the anonymous letter, and (2) independently investigated and corroborated some of the allegations in that letter. For example, assume that the police arrived at the citizen-defendant's house because of a *hunch*, or because they just did not like him. Without the anonymous letter or the subsequent investigation of some of the allegations in that letter, is the warrantless entry based on a third-party consent constitutional?

To determine the constitutionality of the warrantless entry even under our modified hypothetical a judge faces the same query posed to the Supreme Court in its seminal third-party consent opinion:

> Would the facts available to the officers at the moment… warrant a man of reasonable caution in the belief that the consenting party had authority over the premises?

The Court concluded that the facts "*available*" to the officers supported a reasonable (though mistaken) belief that the consenter had the authority to consent. Several key facts available to the officers in the seminal case are not present in either our hypothetical or its modified version.

First, the police in the seminal case met the purported consenter at a time before and at a place other than the defendant's apartment. During this initial encounter with the police the purported consenter told the police that she had been assaulted by the defendant, and that the defendant was presently asleep in that apartment. The purported consenter showed signs of a severe beating. Moreover, she agreed to travel with the police to that apartment and unlock the door with her key.

Second, during the drive to the defendant's apartment the purported consenter several times referred to the apartment as "*our apartment*" and said that she had clothes and furniture there.

Third, the purported consenter unlocked the door to the defendant's apartment with a key.

Even *with* the anonymous letter and the subsequent investigation the warrantless entry based on third-party consent in our hypothetical lacks the factual support for a reasonable belief compared to the facts in the seminal case. Suffice it to say the factual support in the modified hypothetical is weaker still.

Third-Party Consent Actual Authority

In our hypothetical the young woman in the overalls was not the defendant's, "Bob" Sample's, paramour. Moreover, she did not live with Sample. However, in this *variation* on that theme the young woman, Celest Bivens, is not only Sample's paramour but she has also been living with him for the past six months. Although Bivens has shared the two-bedroom 1,800-square-foot house with Sample, her name is not on the mortgage instrument. Even so, she had mutual use and control over all areas of that house except for Bob's private bedroom and his special green footlocker which bore the following words in big red letters *Bob's Special Footlocker.*

When the police officers arrived at Sample's house, Bivens was home alone. One of the officers (Conner) told Bivens about Sample's suspected cocaine enterprise. Officer Conner asked Bivens if she lived in that house, and whether she kept personal effects (clothing, toothbrush, etc.) there. In response, Bivens said "yes, I have been living here for six months." Officer Conner then asked her if he could search the house for narcotics. Again, Bivens said yes. Officer Conner and his fellow officers began to search the house.

During the search of the house Officer Conner and his fellow officers found (1) an ounce of cocaine in the kitchen refrigerator, (2) an ounce of cocaine in a cabinet of the master bathroom, and (3) a pound of cocaine in Sample's special footlocker located in his private (second) bedroom. Sample's motion to exclude all three items of cocaine asserts, among other things, that the three items should be excluded from his trial because Officer Conner and his fellow officers violated Sample's Fourth Amendment rights. As a result, Sample argues that the seized cocaine is excludable as fruits of the poisonous tree (Fruits of that Fourth Amendment violation). In order to determine whether to admit or exclude this evidence (items of cocaine) the trial judge must examine Bivens's purported consent under the *third-party* consent law where the citizen (Bivens) had actual authority to consent.

The cocaine retrieved from the kitchen refrigerator and from the master bathroom should not be excluded primarily because these two searches/seizures are lawful under third-party consent law. That is, the consent of a person (Bivens)

> Who possesses common authority over premises or effects is valid as against the absent, nonconsenting person with whom that authority is shared.

More important, the Supreme Court warned that this common authority does not rest on a third party's (Bivens) mere property interest. Instead, the common authority of a third party rests on mutual use of the property by persons generally having joint access or control for most purposes, so that it is reasonable to recognize that any of the co-inhabitants has the right to permit the inspection in his own right and that the others have assumed the risk that one of their number might permit the common area to be searched. In this variation ((b)) of the hypothetical the consenting third party (Bivens) possesses actual authority to consent to Officer's Conner's search of *common* areas of the house. Therefore, the *absent* (asleep) non-consenting person

(Sample) has *assumed the risk* that the person with whom he shares possession and authority of the premises will permit someone else (including the police) to search the premises. Furthermore, any evidence discovered pursuant to this third-party consent search is admissible against the absent non-consenting person, Bob Sample. Although the Supreme Court's seminal decision clearly provides that persons sharing mutual authority over the premises "assume the risk" that his/her roommate will permit another (thc police?) to search the premises, it has not precisely defined how a container found within mutually shared property is to be treated.

One commentator has concluded that the Court's seminal opinion on third-party consent by a person with actual authority fails to consider the more precise issue of whether the bag within which the [evidence] was found was jointly used "and instead focused solely on whether" "there was generally a sharing of the bedroom."

Courts and legal commentators have further concluded that a protected expectation of privacy may exist where the defendant has taken some special steps to protect his personal effects from the scrutiny of others, but does not unquestionably exist where the co-occupant has ready access to the place searched.

Consistent with these principles in this version of our facts, Sample has taken "special steps to *protect* his personal effects from the scrutiny of others." He had a separate (from the master bedroom) private bedroom that Bivens acknowledged. Moreover, inside that private bedroom Sample had a closed green footlocker that conspicuously indicated (red lettering) the contents of the locker (or its use) were for his eyes only. So, Bivens did not have actual authority to grant the police permission to search either the private bedroom or the contents (the green footlocker) of that private bedroom. Hence, a search of either the private bedroom or the green footlocker was *unreasonable*.

Third-Party Consent Actual Authority Trumped by a Present and Objecting Co-occupant

In our hypothetical the young woman in overalls was not the defendant's/Bob Sample's paramour. Moreover, she did not live with Sample. However, in this *variation* on that theme the woman clad in overalls, Celest Bivens, is not only Sample's paramour but has also been living with him for the past six months. Although Bivens has shared the two- bedroom 1,800-square-foot house with Sample, her name is not on the mortgage instrument. Even so, she had mutual use and control over all areas of that house.

When the police arrived at Sample's house, Bivens was standing on the front porch. Sample was asleep in the master bedroom. Officer Conner asked Bivens if she lived in that house, and whether she kept personal effects (clothing, toothbrush, etc.) there. In response Bivens said, "yes, I have been living here with Bob for the past six months. If you don't believe me go ask Bob—he's in the master bedroom sound asleep." Officer Conner said, "I believe you, but I have important police work to do. Do you mind if I search your house for narcotics and such?" Without a pause Bivens said "yes, you can." Officer Conner and his fellow officers started to enter the house.

Before Officer Conner and his men could enter the house Sample met them at the door. He said, "I object to you entering my house without a warrant!" Fortuitously (for him) Sample had awakened to hear Bivens granting Conner and his men permission to enter. Officer Conner told Sample that he could not veto Bivens's consent for them to enter. According to Officer Conner the law allowed the police to enter the home of roommates upon the voluntary consent of any one of the roommates. As a result, Officer Conner concluded that the objection of the co-occupant had no effect on the consenting roommate's permission for the police to enter. With that rejection of Sample's purported objection to their entry Officer Conner and his fellow officers entered the house and began the search. During the search the police officers found (1) an ounce of cocaine in the kitchen refrigerator, (2) a pound of cocaine in a cabinet of the master bedroom, and (3) two pounds of cocaine under the master bed. Sample's motion to exclude all three items of cocaine asserts, among other things, that the three items should be excluded from his trial because Officer Conner and his fellow officers ignored his specific objection not to enter his house. Therefore, Sample argues that his Fourth Amendment rights were violated, and the found items of cocaine are excludable as fruits of the poisonous tree. In order to determine whether to admit or exclude this evidence (three items of cocaine), the trial judge must examine whether the police must honor a co-occupant's objection to his fellow roommate's consent for the police to enter shared premises.

In *Georgia v. Radolph*, the United States Supreme Court has held that the Fourth Amendment recognizes a valid warrantless entry and search of premises when police obtain the voluntary consent of an occupant who shares, or is reasonably believed to share, authority over the area in common with a co-occupant who later objects to the use of evidence so obtained. However, the question *here*, in our newly created variation, is the same as that in the seminal Supreme Court opinion: whether such an evidentiary seizure is likewise lawful with the permission of one occupant when the other, who later seeks to suppress the evidence, is present at the scene and expressly refuses to consent.

The Supreme Court directly held as follows: "We hold that, in the circumstances here at issue, a physically present co-occupant's stated refusal to permit entry prevails, rendering the warrantless search unreasonable and invalid as to him." In essence, the Court has concluded that as the co-tenant wishing to open the door to a third party has no recognized authority in law or social practice to permit over a present and objecting co-tenant, his disputed invitation, without more, gives a police officer no better claim to reasonableness in entering than the officer would have in the absence of any consent at all.

So, under our variation of the hypothetical the trial judge should exclude all three items of cocaine because the physically present co-occupant's refusal to permit the police a warrantless entry *trumps* his roommate's consent. Even in our variation of the hypothetical, however, the Court has held that a co-occupant is not present if he is (1) asleep inside (or nearby) the house, or (2) awake (inside or outside the house) but unaware that his roommate has given consent to the police. Moreover, the police are not required to take affirmative steps to make a co-occupant aware before they enter pursuant to the co-occupant's roommate's consent. On the other hand, the police may not remove the potentially objecting co-occupant from the premises to insure that he cannot object.

EXCEPTIONS TO THE WARRANT REQUIREMENT

5

OPENING REMARKS

A search or seizure conducted without a warrant is presumptively unreasonable. However, a warrantless entry may be reasonable if based on exceptional circumstances. An exceptional circumstance occurs when there are exigent circumstances in which to preserve the evidence of the crime police action literally must be now or never. In other words, under exigent circumstances it is permissible for the police to act without prior judicial approval.

Now-or-never searches have included warrantless entry (1) to a suspect's home due to exigent circumstances, (2) to provide emergency aid, (3) to search a readily mobile automobile, and (4) to conduct searches and seizures for evidence that is in imminent danger of destruction. Although exigent circumstances are not limited to the Fourth Amendment, these four examples of exigent circumstances in the Fourth Amendment context will be examined in turn.

Warrantless Entry into a Citizen's Home Based on Exigent Circumstances

In *Warden, Maryland Penitentiary v. Hayden,* the Supreme Court recognized that when the police had probable cause to believe that an armed robber had entered a house a few minutes before the police arrived, it was reasonable for the police to make a warrantless entry into that house, to arrest the suspect, and to search for weapons. Although the Court stated that the exigent situation made the warrantless search imperative, the Court did not specify the elements of the exigency, except the Court did state that where the circumstances pose dangers for citizens or the police and speed is essential, exigent circumstances supported by probable cause justify a warrantless entry. Apparently, knowledge that a suspected armed robber had recently entered a house posed sufficient danger, and speed was essential to neutralize that danger.

Warrantless Entry to Provide Emergency Aid

The Fourth Amendment does not bar police officers from making warrantless entries and searches when they reasonably believe that a person within is in need of immediate aid. However, a warrantless search must be justified by a specific exigency. In other words, the Court has found that a prompt warrantless search to aid possible victims at a homicide scene is reasonable. The Court has, however, rejected as unreasonable a four-day warrantless search of a homicide scene as an emergency search. That is, the Court rejected a categorical emergency exception at a homicide scene. Exigent circumstances must be evaluated in each instance.

Although the Court has held that warrantless searches and seizures inside a home without a warrant are presumptively unreasonable, it has also concluded that this presumption can be overcome. Moreover, when the emergency arises the emergency aid exception does not depend on the officers' subjective intent. The exigencies of the situation may make the needs of law enforcement so compelling that a warrantless search is objectively reasonable. For example, a warrantless search is objectively reasonable when the officer has a need to assist persons who are seriously injured or who are threatened with serious injury. And, even if the occupant-owner of the home specifically objects to the police entry, the Court has held that it was objectively reasonable for the officer to (1) enter the premises to protect the objecting citizen, and (b) presume that the objecting citizen's violent acts of throwing projectiles might harm another unseen (or unheard) human target.

Exigency Exception—Invalid (*Kentucky v. King*)

Although the Court has consistently held that searches and seizures inside a home without a warrant are presumptively unreasonable, it has also held that this presumption may be overcome when the "exigencies of the situation make the needs of law enforcement so compelling that [a] warrantless search is objectively reasonable under The Fourth Amendment" [quoting *Mincey v. Arizona*].

However, under what has been called the police created exigency exigent circumstances do not justify a warrantless search when the exigency was created or manufactured by the conduct of the police. The *King* Court devised a test to determine whether the police had manufactured an exigency. According to this test, a warrantless entry based on exigent circumstances is reasonable when the police did not create the exigency by engaging in or threatening to engage in conduct that violates the Fourth Amendment.

Warrantless Search of a Movable Car

The so-called automobile exception allows the police to conduct a warrantless search of a car under exigent circumstances. Where the police have probable cause that an automobile contains contraband, but it is not practical for the police to secure a warrant, the police may conduct a warrantless search of that automobile because the vehicle can be quickly moved out of the locality or jurisdiction in which the warrant must be sought, *Carroll v. United States.*

The main rationale for permitting a warrantless search of an automobile is that automobiles are readily movable, and the opportunity for a search is fleeting. Although the Court cited *Carroll* (so-called automobile exception), it held in *Chambers v. Maroney* that the automobile could only be lawfully searched (1) without a warrant if the search was conducted at the scene of the stop, or (2) with a warrant where the search was conducted at the police station. Unfortunately, the *Chambers* Court did not adopt either option. Instead, without explanation the Court approved of a warrantless search at the police station.

After *Chambers,* the Court has developed another justification for permitting the warrantless search of a car based on the automobile exception. In *Cardwell v. Lewis,* the Court determined that a citizen has a lesser expectation of privacy in a car. According to the Court, the function of an automobile is transportation, and that it seldom serves as one's residence or as the repository of personal effects.

Even so, the Court acknowledged that a citizen does not lose Fourth Amendment protection to all of a car's interior just because he exercised his right to be mobile.

Under this *lesser expectation of privacy* rationale, it is permissible for the police to conduct a warrantless removal of paint scrapings from the exterior of a citizen's car. Litigants citing *Cardwell* and its *diminished expectations* rationale should take note that the Court distinguished an automobile's interior (entitled to protection of at least those areas not exposed to public view) from its exterior (not entitled to protection).

The Court has extended the automobile exception to motor homes because a motor home is more like an automobile than a home. Although this exception relied on the ready mobility of the vehicle and on the presence of the vehicle in a setting that objectively indicates that the vehicle is being used for transportation, it curiously implied that the automobile exception may apply to a vehicle even if that vehicle is situated in a way or place that objectively indicates that it is being used as a residence. Again, the Court does not explain.

The So-Called Automobile Exception and Containers

Based on Court precedents and the record in the case, the *Carroll* Court concluded that the federal prohibition agents had justification for the *search* and *seizure* of the Oldsmobile Roadster automobile. That is, the Court held

> [t]hat the facts and circumstances within their knowledge and of which they had reasonably trustworthy information were sufficient in themselves to warrant a man of reasonable caution in the belief that intoxicating liquor was being transported in the automobile they stopped and searched.

During the search of that automobile, the Court reported that one of the federal agents tore open a cushion of a car seat in that automobile. Inside that torn seat cushion, the agent found two bottles of illicit liquor. As federal agents were allowed to tear open the seat in a car in order to retrieve illicit liquor, *Carroll*, presumably, allowed the government to search anywhere inside a car where the object of that search could reasonably be found. Despite the apparent logic of this position, the issue of whether it was reasonable for federal agents to conduct a warrantless search of a *container* found in a car during a *Carroll* search was unclear. The *scope* of a *Carroll* search was primarily unclear because the Court (after *Carroll*) had developed two lines of authority concerning warrantless searches and seizures of automobiles versus warrantless searches and seizures of movable containers, *United States v. Chadwick* and *Arkansas v. Sanders*.

Unlike *Carroll*, both *United States v. Chadwick* and *Arkansas v. Sanders* concerned police officers who had probable cause to believe that narcotics were stowed in a particular container (a foot locker in *Chadwick*, a green suitcase in *Sanders*), but the officers did not have probable cause to search the automobiles in which the containers were later placed.

> It was the luggage being transported by respondent at the time of the arrest, not the automobile in which it was being carried, that was the suspected locus of the contraband. The relationship between the automobile in which it was being carried was purely coincidental, as in Chadwick.

In finding that the footlocker in *Chadwick* and the suitcase in *Sanders* were protected from a warrantless search, the Court emphasized the importance of the Fourth

Amendment privacy interests when citizens place private effects in a repository designed to protect privacy. Similarly, the Court rejected comparing the search of a footlocker or a suitcase with the warrantless search of an automobile. First, the Court observed that in the *automobile exception*, cars have been treated differently because of inherent mobility, which often makes obtaining a warrant impracticable. Besides, in both cases the government had the footlocker and the suitcase under its control and it had time to obtain a warrant.

Second, neither the owner of the footlocker nor the owner of the suitcase had lost their expectation of privacy by placing their container in an automobile parked at the curb or in one stopped after driving away from the curb:

> [A] suitcase taken from an automobile stopped on the highway is not necessarily attended by any lesser expectation of privacy than is associated with luggage taken from any other place.

The Court did, however, carve out an exception to *Chadwick's* and *Sanders's* expectation of privacy in closed containers:

> Not all containers and packages found by police during the course of a search will deserve the full protection of the Fourth Amendment. Thus, some containers (for example a kit of burglar tools or a gun case) by their very nature cannot support any reasonable expectation of privacy because their contents can be inferred from their outward appearance.

In any event, *Chadwick/Sanders* permit the warrantless *seizure* of a container, but the *search* (unlike in *Carroll*) must be conducted pursuant to a warrant. So, the *Chadwick/Sanders* line of authority differs from the *Carroll* line.

In *United States v. Ross*, the Court addressed the issue of a warrantless search of a container found inside a car during a lawful search under the automobile exception. The *Ross* Court concluded that it was a recognized exception to the warrant requirement for the police to conduct a warrantless search of an automobile when the police have probable cause that the automobile contains contraband. After noting that *Carroll* was a recognized exception to the warrant requirement, *Ross* announced that it was required to determine the scope of a *Carroll* search. The *Ross* Court distinguished the warrantless search and seizure of a container under *Chadwick/Sanders* from the warrantless search and seizure of an automobile in *Carroll*. It found that *Chadwick/Sanders* required the police to have probable cause as to the particular container. On the other hand, *Carroll* required the police to have probable cause as to the automobile.

After *Ross,* the two lines of legal precedents regarding the warrantless search and seizure of containers was firmly established. *Chadwick/Sanders* allowed the police, who had probable cause as to a container, to seize the container without a warrant, but required the police to obtain a warrant before conducting a search. However, the *Carroll/Ross* line of authority allowed the police, who had probable cause to believe that an automobile contained contraband, to search and seize that automobile without a warrant. Moreover, the *Carroll/Ross* exception to the warrant requirement allowed the police to search every part of the vehicle and its contents that may conceal the object of the search. The Court, however, recognizes that the police may not hold a car indefinitely before conducting a search. Nor are the police immune from a lawsuit by a citizen claiming that an unreasonable delay in the search adversely affected a privacy or possessory interest.

After *Ross,* a citizen's expectation of privacy in closed personal luggage placed in an automobile is less protected under the Fourth Amendment warrant requirement. According to *Ross*, when the police have probable cause to believe that an automobile contains contraband they may conduct a warrantless search of that vehicle and any containers in it that could reasonably hold that contraband. Presumably this expansion of the automobile exception to include containers found in the vehicle was inspired by the Court's desire to assist the police in performing their jobs more efficiently. However, this position in *Ross* contradicts the Court's long-established Fourth Amendment jurisprudence that insuring efficient police action is never sufficient to abandon the Fourth Amendment warrant requirement.

Conflating *Chadwick/Sanders* into *Carroll/Ross*

In *Chadwick/Sanders* the police had probable cause to search a container. Hence, the police were allowed to conduct a warrantless seizure of the container. But they had to secure a warrant to conduct a search. However, under the automobile exception, the police must have probable cause to believe that the automobile contains contraband. In the automobile exception cases, the police with probable cause to search a car may conduct a warrantless search of any part of that car that could reasonably hold the object of the search, including closed containers. Invariably, the Court had interpreted these two lines as separate and distinct legal precedents. However, in 1991 the Court in *California v. Acevedo* concluded that it had to re-examine the law applicable to a closed container in an automobile, because the Court determined that this was a subject that had troubled courts and law enforcement officers since it was first considered in *Chadwick*. The Court cited no authority for this conclusion.

The *Acevedo* Court claimed that the *Chadwick/Sanders* rule had confused courts and police and had impeded effective law enforcement. The alleged lack of clarity between *Carroll/Ross* and *Chadwick/Sanders* was one of the reasons given by the *Acevedo* Court for concluding that it was better to adopt one clear-cut rule to govern automobile searches and eliminate the warrant requirement for closed containers set forth in *Sanders*. After *Acevedo*, it appears that once the police have probable cause to search a container and that container is placed in a car, then the police may conduct a warrantless search and seizure of that container. *Chadwick/Sanders* has been overruled—at least when the container has been placed in an automobile. On the other hand, the police may not search the remainder of the car unless they have probable cause to believe contraband or evidence is contained in that part of the car.

HYPOTHETICAL

Police Chief Marck Jackson (hereafter "Chief Jackson") of the Fayetteberg Police Department found the following anonymous letter under his office door around 7:30 am on May 29, 2004:

> I am an employee at Wal-Market Super Center on 12th Street in Fayetteberg. You should know that several people on the Wal-Market management staff at this store are selling powdered cocaine to kids at Fayetteberg High School and Romney Jr.

> High. Two kids at Romney Jr. High died from overdosing on this toxic dope. The street name of this cocaine is "Triple H."
>
> By the way, some of these Wal-Market managers are quite well-known in the community. Two of them are named "Bob." You know them well! They brag on how they've made so much money selling drugs and how they can hide it through their regular jobs. They sell the cocaine from a big red grocery bag with a big white X marked on two sides of that bag.

Chief Jackson conducted a search of police files to determine if any students from Romney Jr. High had recently died of toxic drugs. After a two-hour search he found records of three recent deaths by toxic drugs. Two of these deaths were of seventh graders at Canal Jr. High. The other death was of an eighth grader at Romney Jr. High. He also had several tips from other reliable informants that "Bob" Sample sold drugs in the neighborhood from his red grocery bag.

After this search, Chief Jackson called the Wal-Market Home Office in Collierville. Chief Jackson identified himself and asked the appropriate personnel to locate the full name and address of the manager, "Jim Bob," at the 12th Street Super Center. After a ninety-minute search, the Home Office confirmed that there were two employee-managers at that store named "Bob." "Jim Bob" Sample was not only in his seventh year as a manager, but he was also a popular country-western singer in the Ozarks, and James Robert ("Bob") Powell was a two-year veteran and a popular thespian in a local theater troupe. "Bob" Powell, however, was on duty at a Wal-Market in China. So, Chief Jackson dispatched six officers to "Bob" Sample's home at 2342 Dayton Place.

Chief Jackson's team of six officers was led by Officer Frank Pendleton. Officer Pendleton was a ten-year veteran. When Pendleton and his team arrived at 2342 Dayton Place they discovered that they could not observe, from ground level, a greenhouse located in the backyard of the property nor could they see any other aspects of the house except for a fully appointed triple-white automobile parked behind a gate in a private driveway. The automobile was registered to Robert and Amanda Powell. They were not able to see any exterior details of the house or the greenhouse because the rest of the property was almost totally enclosed by a ten-foot-high oak paneled fence that had several "DO NOT ENTER" signs written in red ink posted at each corner. However, part of the wall consisted of a four-foot high see-through wire fence that covered the private driveway. This gate was locked. Despite these obstacles Officer Pendleton persevered. Indeed, he was able to view (and record the license plate number) of all the people who drove up to the metal-and-oak door built into the ten-foot oak fence. His written report (and the subsequent affidavit) noted that this door had an obvious peephole in its center. During a two-hour observation period Officer Pendleton and his team of officers observed and noted six cars drive up to the metal-and-oak gate door. Although each car contained several occupants only the occupant in the front passenger seat emerged from the car and walked toward the door.

The officers observed that each time a "visitor" rang the gate door's bell a man would emerge from the door carrying a large red grocery bag with a white X on two sides. The man who emerged from behind the door fit the description of "Bob" Sample provided by the informant. Sample engaged each "visitor" in the same manner. That is, he gave each visitor a robust handshake, a hug, and a small brown paper bag taken from the large red paper bag. In return for the small brown paper bag the "visitor" would place a small bundle of U.S. currency in Bob's hand. When the seventh passenger approached the gate door, Officer Pendleton signaled for his team to move in. The moment after Sample handed the seventh "visitor" the small brown paper bag, and the "visitor" handed him a small bundle of U.S. currency, Pendleton and his team moved in.

Officer Pendleton yelled, "Freeze, you with the red bag! Don't anybody move.' " Instead of "freezing" Sample hurriedly stuck the red bag through the wire fence and into the passenger side window of the white automobile. Bob placed the red bag in the *far left corner* under the dashboard. Then Sample "froze". Pendleton stepped close to Sample and told him not to move. As the wire fence was locked, Officer Pendleton reached inside the automobile and seized a black-and-white leather pouch lying in the *far right corner* (passenger side window) under the dashboard. Written on that leather pouch were these words: "This pouch belongs to Bob Sample of 2342 Dayton Place." After seizing the leather pouch Officer Pendleton opened it. Inside the pouch Officer Pendleton found a list of Sample's drug sales for the previous two weeks, $15,000 cash (in small and large bills), and a DVD. On the DVD were several scenes of Sample committing two graphic murders (gun shot) and smiling into the camera while saying these words: "Yeah, I killed them both. That's what happens when you try to steal my territory!" A subsequent search of Sample's backyard pursuant to a search warrant resulted in the discovery of two bodies buried in shallow graves.

An arraignment has been set. At that arraignment Sample will request that all the evidence uncovered during these searches and seizures be excluded as "fruits" of Fourth Amendment violations.

Defendant has filed a motion-in-limine to suppress contraband and other incriminating evidence discovered during a warrantless search and seizure. You are an associate prosecutor. Please provide your senior prosecutor with a memorandum of law (1) analyzing the key legal precedents that the defendant will likely use to support his motions, (2) isolating the most persuasive arguments distilled from those precedents, and (3) predicting how the court is likely to rule on these competing arguments.

LIST OF READINGS

1. The Fourth Amendment to the United States Constitution.
2. Federal Rules of Evidence Rule 401. Definition of Relevant Evidence.
3. Federal Rules of Evidence Rule 402. Relevant Evidence Generally Admissible; Irrelevant Evidence Inadmissible.
4. *Katz v. United States*, 389 U.S. 347 (1967).
5. *Roaden v. Kentucky*, 413 U.S. 496 (1973).
6. *Mincey v. Arizona*, 437 U.S. 385, 394 (1978).
7. *Chambers v. Maroney*, 399 U.S. 42 (1970).
8. *Warden, Maryland Penitentiary v. Hayden*, 387 U.S. 294 (1967).
9. *United States v. Santana*, 427 U.S. 38 (1976).
10. *Brigham City v. Stuart*, 547 U.S. 398 (2006).
11. *Carroll v. United States*, 267 U.S. 132 (1925).
12. *United States v. Ross*, 456 U.S. 798 (1982).
13. *California v. Carney*, 471 U.S. 386 (1985).
14. *Ker v. California*, 374 U.S. 23 (1963).
15. *New York v. Quarles*, 467 U.S. 649 (1984).
16. *Michigan v. Fisher*, 130 S. Ct. 546 (2009).

17. *Groh v. Ramirez*, 540 U.S. 551 (2004).
18. *Cardwell v. Lewis*, 417 U.S. 583 (1974).
19. *California v. Acevedo*, 500 U.S. 565 (1991).
20. *United States v. Chadwick*, 433 U.S. 1 (1977).
21. *Arkansas v. Sanders*, 442 U.S. 753 (1979).
22. *Wyoming v. Houghton*, 526 U.S. 295 (1999).
23. *Zurcher v. Stanford Daily*, 436 U.S. 547 (1978).
24. *United States v. Johns*, 469 U.S. 478 (1985).
25. Yale Kamisar, The "Automobile Search" Cases: The Court Does Little to Clarify the "Labyrinth" of Judicial Uncertainty, in 3 Supreme Court: Trends and Developments 1980–81, p. 69 (D. Opperman ed. 1982).
26. *Kentucky v. King*, 131 S. Ct. 1849 (2011).

SAMPLE ESSAY

To: Senior Prosecutor
From: Associate Prosecutor
Re: Pretrial Proceedings—Defendant's motion-in-limine to suppress contraband and other incriminating evidence discovered during a warrantless search and seizure
Date:

In anticipation of the upcoming motion-in-limine by the defendant described above, I have prepared the following memorandum identifying and explaining some of the key issues involved in this matter. Essentially the defendant will argue that the police, without a warrant, entered his automobile, seized, and searched his black-and-white leather pouch. He will contend that this warrantless search and seizure violated his Fourth Amendment rights. Then, he will argue that all of the incriminating evidence discovered because of that warrantless search and seizure must be excluded. In response, we should argue that *California v. Acevedo* held, among other things, that the police may search an automobile and the containers within it where they have probable cause that the car contains contraband. According to *Acevedo* the warrantless search and seizure of defendant's leather pouch was constitutional.

Since *Acevedo* and the opinions predating it will form the core of our argument this memorandum will articulate the fundamentals of *Acevedo* and how those fundamentals support the police action in this scenario. Of course, if we fail to show the *reasonableness* of this warrantless police action the court will likely exclude all of the evidence found in defendant's leather pouch. Accordingly, if this incriminating evidence is excluded from the defendant's trial the court will dismiss the charges against him. In any event, my analysis of how we may prevail is set out more particularly below.

PART A. THE GENERAL RULE OF ADMISSIBILITY

Federal Rule of Evidence 401 provides that all relevant evidence is admissible except as otherwise provided by the Constitution of the United States. Because the Fourth Amendment to the United States Constitution prohibits unreasonable searches and seizures, any unreasonable search or seizure violates the Fourth Amendment. For example, the Supreme Court has held that a warrantless search of a citizen's property by an agent of the government violates the Fourth Amendment. More important, in order to make this Fourth Amendment protection effective the Supreme Court has held that evidence seized as a result of the unlawful search could not constitute proof at trial against the victim of the search.

During the pretrial proceedings I anticipate that the defendant will initially argue that it is a cardinal principle that warrantless searches are per se unreasonable under the Fourth Amendment. However he must also acknowledge that this cardinal principle is subject to a few specifically established and well-delineated exceptions. The most applicable exceptions to our facts are the venerable *Carroll* doctrine and the more recently adopted test in *California v. Acevedo*.

Carroll, he will argue, applies only where the police have probable cause that an automobile contains contraband. He will inform the judge that the police in this case had reason to believe that the red grocery bag, a container, not the automobile, contained contraband. When the police have probable cause that a container holds contraband the governing case precedents are *United States v. Chadwick* and *Arkansas v. Sanders*. *Chadwick* and *Sanders*, he will argue, only allow the police to conduct a warrantless seizure. Once the police have effected the warrantless seizure and taken the container under their control, he will assert that *Sanders* provides that, as a general rule, there is no greater need for warrantless searches of luggage taken from automobiles than of luggage taken from other places. And, then to emphasize why he is entitled to an order of exclusion, the defendant will cite this cogent excerpt from *Chadwick*: "With the footlocker safely immobilized, it was unreasonable to undertake the additional and greater intrusion of a search without a warrant."

Ordinarily, defendant's arguments would be highly persuasive, if not dispositive. However, these arguments are neither if *Chadwick* and *Sanders* do not apply. We should contend that our facts are controlled by *California v. Acevedo*, not *Chadwick-Sanders*. As a result, the bright-line rule adopted in *Acevedo* overruled *Chadwick* and *Sanders:* "We conclude that it is better to adopt one clear-cut rule to govern automobile searches and eliminate the warrant requirement for closed containers set forth in *Sanders*." That clear-cut rule adopted by the *Acevedo* Court was stated as follows: "We therefore interpret *Carroll* as providing one rule to govern all automobile searches. The police may search an automobile and the containers within it when they have probable cause to believe contraband or evidence is contained." As *Acevedo* overrules *Chadwick-Sanders* we should prevail at this pretrial proceeding. The incriminating evidence should not be subject to the exclusionary rule.

TOOLS FOR SELF-CRITICISM

The state's contention that *California v. Acevedo* controls the facts of this hypothetical is problematic. First, *Acevedo* concerned probable cause as to a particular container (brown paper bag) before it was placed in the car. In this manner, *Acevedo* tracks *Chadwick-Sanders* probable cause to the container line of cases. Second, the police in our hypothetical did not have probable cause to the leather pouch. Hence, *Acevedo* does not squarely support the state's argument. Nevertheless, the critical language in *Acevedo* regarding a clear-cut rule to cover all containers during an automobile search provides some support for that position. Moreover, this aspect of *Acevedo* has not been fully interpreted.

ARREST IN A PUBLIC PLACE OR ONE'S PRIVATE HOME

6

OPENING REMARKS

Arrest without a Warrant in a *Public Place*

The United States Supreme Court has consistently observed that it is a *cardinal principle* that warrantless searches are per se unreasonable under the Fourth Amendment. However, the Court has recognized that this *cardinal principle* is subject to a few specifically established and well-delineated exceptions. One such delineated exception is that the Fourth Amendment does not require a warrant to make a valid arrest for a felony offense. Indeed, the Court has observed that

> The usual rule is that a police officer may arrest without warrant one believed by the officer upon reasonable cause to have been guilty of a felony....

In *Watson v. United States*, the Supreme Court held that a federal statute authorizing postal workers to conduct warrantless arrests based on probable cause constituted a legislative judgment that such warrantless arrests are reasonable.

Furthermore, according to the *Watson* Court

> The necessary inquiry, therefore, was not whether there was a warrant or whether there was time to get one, but whether there was probable cause for the arrest.

After *Atwater v. City of Lago Vista*, the Court confirmed what its prior cases suggested that a police officer who has probable cause to believe that a citizen has committed a very minor offense (misdemeanor) in his presence may arrest that citizen without a warrant.

In any event, the Court held that the standard of probable cause applies to all arrests, without the need to balance the interests and circumstances in particular situations. Accordingly, the Court concluded that

> If an officer has probable cause to believe that an individual has committed even a very minor criminal offense in his presence, he may, without violating the Fourth Amendment, arrest the offender.

Although the Court considered Atwater's arrest humiliating, it did not find that the arrest was conducted in an *"extraordinary manner, unusually harmful to [her] privacy or... physical interests"*. That is, it was not so extraordinary as to violate the Fourth Amendment.

Atwater confirmed that whenever a police officer has probable cause to believe that a citizen has committed even a minor criminal offense in his presence, that officer may conduct a warrantless arrest of that citizen. Employing reasoning from a previous case the *Atwater* Court determined that the reasonableness of a warrantless arrest based on probable cause did not require it to weigh the governmental or the individual's interests. Similarly, in *Whren v. United States* where a warrantless traffic stop was based on probable cause, the Court held that it need not determine reasonableness by considering whether such a stop made by plainclothes officers in unmarked cars violated police regulations. Moreover, the Court opined that the reasonableness of a warrantless traffic stop need not be determined by considering the motivations of the officers who conducted the stop.

Therefore, where a police officer has probable cause that a citizen has committed a criminal offense (no matter how minor), the police may arrest without *balancing* (governmental and individual interests) costs and benefits or without determining whether the arrest of the citizen *was in some sense necessary. Balancing*, however, may be appropriate under special circumstances. For example, the Court has held that

> Where probable cause has existed, the only cases in which we have found it necessary actually to perform the balancing analysis involved searches and seizures conducted in an extraordinary manner, unusually harmful to an individual's privacy or even physical interests... such as for example, seizure by means of deadly force or an unannounced entry into a house.

The Court in *Welsh v. Wisconsin* measured a state's interest in conducting a warrantless arrest in a citizen's home by evaluating how the state classified the charged offense: driving while intoxicated. This *first offense* of driving while intoxicated was classified as a non-criminal, civil forfeiture offense where no prison time was possible. Accordingly, the Court opined that

> Given this expression of the State's interest, a warrantless home arrest cannot be upheld simply because evidence of the petitioner's blood-alcohol level might have dissipated while the police obtained a warrant. To allow a warrantless home entry on these facts would be to approve unreasonable police behavior that the principles of the Fourth Amendment will not sanction.

On the other hand, the Court has held that the police did not act unreasonably under the Fourth Amendment by making a warrantless arrest for a misdemeanor traffic violation where an arrest was prohibited by state law. In *Virginia v. Moore*, the police arrested Moore for driving on a suspended license, even though Virginia law only empowered the police to issue a summons for that offense. The question presented to the Court was whether a police officer violates the Fourth Amendment by making an arrest that is based on probable cause but is prohibited by state law. Of course, the only reason this matter had to be considered by the Court was because the subsequent search incident to Moore's arrest revealed that he was carrying sixteen grams of crack cocaine and cash. As a result, he was charged with possessing cocaine with the intent to distribute it in violation of Virginia law.

Although Virginia law did not, as a general matter, require suppression of evidence obtained in violation of state law, Moore argued that the Fourth Amendment required suppression. The Court disagreed by emphasizing that

> A state is free to prefer one search-and-seizure policy among the range of constitutionally permissible options, but its choice of a more restrictive option does not render the less restrictive ones unreasonable, and hence unconstitutional.

Based on this analysis, the Court concluded as follows:

> Warrantless arrests for crimes committed in the presence of an arresting officer are reasonable under the Constitution, and that while States are free to regulate such arrests however they desire, state restrictions do not alter the Fourth Amendment's protections.

Consequently, state law forbade Moore's arrest, not the Constitution. The Court acknowledged that an unconstitutional arrest may lead to the exclusion of the evidence seized pursuant to a search incident to arrest. However, the Court noted that it was not the province of the Fourth Amendment to enforce state law. As the arrest was constitutionally reasonable under the Fourth Amendment, the seized evidence was not subject to exclusion.

In another part of its opinion, the *Moore* Court corrected the Virginia Supreme Court's interpretation of a United States Supreme Court precedent, *Knowles v. Iowa*. The Virginia Supreme Court concluded that *Knowles* required the State of Virginia to exclude the evidence found on Moore during the search incident to his arrest because the arrest was unconstitutional as the police *should have* issued a citation instead of making an arrest. The Virginia Supreme Court misread *Knowles*. *Knowles* involved probable cause to issue a citation, but the issuing officer also conducted a *full search* incident to issuing the citation. As *Knowles* did not involve a search incident to an arrest, the *Knowles* Court found that search unconstitutional for failing to satisfy either of the *twin rationales* for the search-incident-to-arrest exception. The *search incident* to the officer's issuance of a citation was unconstitutional in *Knowles*. However, a *search incident* to an arrest based on probable cause was constitutional in *Moore*. Although a *search incident* to a lawful arrest may be constitutional, the *manner* of the search may be unconstitutional.

Seizing a Citizen in an Unreasonable Manner

In *Tennessee v. Garner*, the Court held that it was an unconstitutional use of deadly force for a police officer to shoot and kill a fleeing but unarmed burglary suspect merely to prevent his escape. The Court concluded that

> The use of deadly force to prevent the escape of all felony suspects, whatever, the circumstances, is constitutionally unreasonable.

The Court opined that the reasonableness of a seizure is measured not only by the probable cause shown to support the seizure, but by *how that seizure is made*.

The Court emphasized that it had, in many of its cases, balanced the extent of the intrusion against the need for it in order to determine the reasonableness of the *manner* in which a search or seizure is conducted. Although the Court's *balancing test* did not support the reasonableness of the government's actions in *Tennessee v. Garner*, that Court did provide a general standard for when deadly force might be appropriate:

> Where the officer has probable cause to believe that the suspect poses a threat of serious physical harm, either to the officer or to others, it is not constitutionally unreasonable to prevent escape by using deadly force. Thus, if the suspect threatens the officer with a weapon or there is probable cause to believe that he has committed a crime involving the infliction or threatened infliction of serious physical harm, deadly force may be used if necessary.

Despite the specific language in *Garner*, suggesting that the reasonable use of *deadly force* could be determined by certain preconditions, the Court has declined to adopt this approach in other contexts.

In *Scott v. Harris*, the Court emphatically rejected an attempt to craft an easy-to-apply legal test by using *Garner*'s preconditions to determine the reasonableness of police actions to stop a fleeing motorist during a high speed chase. The Court observed that *Garner* was limited to its facts and not even applicable to car chases in general. Instead, in this high speed car chase scenario, the Court announced that the reasonableness of the police action must be determined by

> Slosh[ing] our way through the factbound morass of reasonableness.

So, the Court had to slosh through the facts in order to answer the query:

> Can an officer take actions that place a fleeing motorist at risk of serious injury or death in order to stop the motorist's flight from endangering the lives of innocent bystanders?

Yes, answered the Court.

> A police officer's attempt to terminate a dangerous high-speed car chase that threatens the lives of innocent by-standers does not violate the Fourth Amendment, even when it places the fleeing motorist at risk of serious injury or death.

On the other hand, in *Graham v. Connor*, the Court held that in 42 U.S.C. § 1983 claims based on allegations that the police used excessive force when conducting an arrest or an investigatory stop:

> The reasonableness inquiry in an excessive force case is an objective one: the question is whether the officers' actions are objectively reasonable in light of the facts and circumstances confronting them, without regard to their underlying intent or motivation.

Moreover, the Court held that the reasonableness of a particular use of force must be judged from the perspective of a reasonable officer on the scene, rather than the 20/20 vision of hindsight.

A Neutral Magistrate Must Evaluate Probable Cause for Continued Detention after a Warrantless Arrest

Long before *Watson, Whren,* or *Atwater*, the United States Supreme Court had upheld a warrantless arrest based only on probable cause. Later, however, the Court recognized that a warrantless arrest nullified an individual's right to have a neutral magistrate determine probable cause prior to an arrest. Yet, the Court was also aware that a with-warrant arrest sometimes handicapped legitimate law enforcement. Concerned about this tension between the rights of an arrestee and the realities of law enforcement, the Court established a *practical compromise* to these competing interests. The Court attempted to reconcile these competing interests by deciding the following issue in *Gerstein v. Pugh*:

> [W]hether a person arrested and held for trial under a prosecutor's information is constitutionally entitled to a judicial determination of probable cause for pretrial restraint of liberty.?

The Court held that an arrestee was entitled to such a determination

> Whatever procedure a State may adopt, it must provide a fair and reliable determination of probable cause as a condition for any significant pretrial restraint of liberty and this determination must be made by a judicial officer either before or promptly after arrest.

The task for the Court after *Gerstein* was to define "promptly after arrest."

Although the *Gerstein* Court concluded that the probable cause proceeding would not be an adversarial one, it left the precise contours of the proceeding to the states. Except, however, the Court attempted to clarify the vague *prompt* requirement:

> Taking into account the competing interests articulated in Gerstein, we believe that a jurisdiction that provides judicial determination of probable cause within 48 hours of arrest will, as a general matter comply with this promptness requirement of Gerstein.

The Court hastened to add that even if a probable cause determination occurred within forty-eight hours of arrest, this hearing may nonetheless violate *Gerstein* if the arrested individual can prove that his or her probable cause determination was delayed unreasonably. Unreasonable delays may include (1) delays for the purpose of gathering additional evidence to justify the arrest, (2) a delay motivated by ill will against the arrested individual, or (3) delay for delay's sake.

Recently, in *Corley v. United States*, the Court was required to decide, among other things, whether an arrestee's confession was admissible at trial if it had been given after an *unreasonable delay* in bringing him before a judge. Although the Court's answer to that query is examined more particularly under *Miranda v. Arizona* and its progeny, *Corley* concluded that exclusion was required pursuant to the *McNabb-Mallory* rule.

An Arrest Warrant Is Required to Arrest a Citizen in the Citizen's Own Home

As previously discussed the Supreme Court has held that a warrantless arrest in a public place supported by probable cause is a reasonable arrest under the Fourth Amendment. At the same time, the Court has considered it a basic

> Principle of Fourth Amendment law that searches and seizures inside a man's house without warrant are *per se* unreasonable in the absence of some one of the number of well defined exigent circumstances.

Despite the Court's conclusions about the reasonableness of a warrantless arrest in a public place and the unreasonableness of a warrantless search or seizure inside the home, the Court had not answered

> The still unsettled question... whether and under what circumstances an officer may enter a suspect's home to make a warrantless arrest.

The Court answered this query in the two consolidated cases in *Payton v. New York*. In the first of the two consolidated cases considered in *Payton*, New York City detectives assembled evidence sufficient to establish probable cause to believe that Theodore Payton had murdered the manager of a gas station. Early the following day, six officers went to Payton's apartment in the Bronx, intending to arrest him. When they arrived at his apartment, without a warrant, they knocked on his door. Although light and music emanated from the apartment there was no response to their knock on the metal door. Then, the officers summoned help and used crowbars to enter the apartment. After entering the apartment the police discovered Payton was not there. However, they did find a shell casing that was later admitted into evidence at Payton's murder trial.

In the second case, during an investigation of two armed robberies, New York police officers secured the identity of the suspected robber from his victims in June 1973, and in January 1974 they discovered where he lived. Even so, they did not attempt to arrest him until the middle of March 1974, nor did they obtain an arrest warrant. When the police went to the suspect's, Obie Riddick's, apartment to arrest him, they knocked on the door. Riddick's son opened the door. Through the open door the police could see Riddick sitting in bed covered by a sheet. The police entered the apartment, without a warrant, and placed Riddick under arrest. Before giving him an opportunity to dress, they (claiming to be searching for weapons) opened a chest of drawers two feet away from the bed and found narcotics and related paraphernalia. Riddick was subsequently indicted on narcotics charges. At a suppression hearing, the trial judge held that the warrantless entry was authorized by the revised New York Statute, and that the search of the immediate area was reasonable. The Appellate Division affirmed the denial of the suppression motion.

> The Supreme Court reversed the New York Court of Appeals and held unambiguously that the Fourth Amendment... prohibits the police from making a warrantless and nonconsensual entry into a suspect's home in order to make a routine felony arrest.

In order to reach this conclusion, the Court emphasized that neither history nor the nation's experience required the court to disregard the overriding respect for the sanctity of the home that has been embedded in our traditions since the origins of the Republic. As a result, the Court has generally condemned the government's warrantless entry into a citizen's home to make a felony arrest.

Arresting a citizen in his own home, held the Court, required an arrest warrant based on probable cause and *reason [for the police] to believe the suspect is within.* To reach this conclusion, the Court specifically noted that it did not consider a warrantless entry based on *exigent circumstances*, nor the warrantless entry of a third party's premises to arrest a suspect.

A Search Warrant Is Required to Arrest a Citizen in a Third Party's Home

After its decision in *Payton*, the Court emphasized that

> [i]n terms that apply equally to seizure of property and to seizures of persons, the Fourth Amendment has drawn a firm line at the entrance to the house. Absent exigent circumstances, that threshold may not reasonably be crossed without a warrant.

For example, in *Steagald v. United States*, a Drug Enforcement Agent (DEA) in Detroit, Michigan, was contacted by a confidential informant who suggested that he might be able to locate a federal fugitive (Ricky Lyons) wanted for drug charges. The confidential informant told the Detroit DEA agent that Lyons could be reached during the *next twenty-four hours* at a particular telephone number in Atlanta, Georgia. Forty-eight hours after receiving this information from the informant, the Detroit agent called a fellow DEA agent in Atlanta and gave him the telephone number where Lyons could be reached.

The Atlanta agent secured from the local telephone company the address corresponding to the telephone number obtained from the informant. In addition to the address, the agent discovered that Lyons was the subject of a six-month-old arrest warrant.

Two days after discovering that address, the Atlanta agent accompanied by eleven other officers drove to that address. While at that address, the team of officers did not find Lyons. Instead, the team found Steagald, a resident of that address; a companion outside the residence; and what appeared to be cocaine inside the residence. Believing that they had found cocaine, the team dispatched an officer to secure a *search warrant*. Pursuant to a search authorized by a search warrant, the team found forty-three pounds of cocaine in the residence. Steagald was arrested and indicted on federal drug charges.

Steagald moved to suppress the evidence found in his residence, on the ground that it was illegally obtained because the agents had failed to secure a search warrant before entering the residence. During the suppression hearing, the Atlanta agent conceded that he was not prevented from securing a search warrant, but that he did not secure one because he believed that the arrest warrant was sufficient to justify the entry and search. Agreeing with the agent's belief, the trial court denied the motion to suppress. As a result, the evidence was admitted at Steagald's trial and he was convicted.

On appeal to the Supreme Court, the government (DEA) initially argued that Steagald (petitioner) did not have *an expectation of privacy* in the residence and therefore had no right (standing) to raise an objection about the government's entry to the premises. The Court summarily rejected the government's argument:

> We conclude… that the Government, through its assertions, concessions and acquiescence, has lost its right to challenge petitioner's assertion that he possessed a legitimate expectation of privacy in the searched home.

After disposing of the government's challenge to Steagald's right (standing) to assert a motion to suppress, the Court turned to what it considered a *narrow* question posed in the case:

> Whether an arrest warrant… as opposed to a search warrant… is adequate to protect the Fourth Amendment interests of persons not named in the warrant, when their homes are searched without their consent and in the absence of exigent circumstances.

The purpose of a warrant, noted the Court, was to place a neutral magistrate between the government and a citizen to ensure that sufficient objectivity is employed to weigh the strength of the evidence supporting the government's contemplated action against the individual's interests in protecting his own liberty and the privacy of his home.

Although the Court observed that both an arrest and search warrant serve to subject the probable cause determination of the police to judicial review, it concluded that the interests protected by these two governmental actions were different. An arrest warrant is issued by a magistrate upon a showing that there is probable cause to seize (arrest) a citizen. Therefore, an arrest warrant serves to protect a citizen's interest of not being subjected to an unreasonable seizure.

By contrast, a search warrant is issued because a showing of probable cause has been made that an item to be seized may be found in a particular place. Consequently, a search warrant safeguards a citizen's interests in the privacy of his home and his possessions against an unjustified intrusion. Accordingly, the Court held that the arrest warrant for Lyons did not protect the privacy interests of Steagald. Only a search warrant could adequately protect Steagald's privacy interests. Perhaps, however, an arrest warrant would have been appropriate if the federal agents could show that Lyons had an *expectation of privacy* in Steagald's house. For example, if they could show that Lyons was an *overnight guest*, the police could claim that an arrest warrant would suffice. Pursuant to this analysis, the home of Steagald becomes the home of the arrestee Lyons. Hence, the police may lawfully enter Steagald's home with an arrest warrant for Lyons per *Payton v. New York*. Now, Steagald and Lyon*s* may object (have standing) to the police entry. However, both will lose on the merits if the only claim is that the police needed to secure a *search* warrant in order to lawfully enter. A full decision of standing follows below.

The Victim of a Search or Seizure May Claim the Right to Object to an Unlawful Search or Seizure

As early as 1886, the Supreme Court held that the remedy of exclusion may apply to a Fourth Amendment violation. The Court also determined that only certain persons are entitled to receive the benefit of exclusion. According to the Court, remedies for violations of constitutional rights would be afforded only to a person who *belongs to* the class for whose sake the constitutional protection is given. In *Jones v. United States*, the Court reasoned that this principle properly limited the availability of the exclusionary remedy.

> It is entirely proper to require of one who seeks to challenge the legality of a search as the basis for suppressing relevant evidence that he allege… that he himself was the victim of an invasion of privacy.

In a case where he was prosecuted for violations of federal narcotics laws petitioner Jones had to make such a showing. The statutory provisions under which the petitioner was prosecuted permitted conviction upon proof that the petitioner possessed the narcotics.

The petitioner had been arrested in an apartment by federal narcotics officers, who were executing a warrant to search for narcotics. Once the federal agents found narcotics in the apartment, the petitioner admitted that some of the narcotics belonged to him. He also told the agents that he lived in that apartment. The petitioner moved to suppress the narcotics by claiming that the search warrant was not based on probable cause. The government challenged the petitioner's right to make this motion (standing) because it argued that the petitioner alleged neither ownership of the seized articles nor an interest in the apartment greater than that of an invitee or guest.

The federal district court judge conducted a hearing to determine petitioner's standing to object to the search of that apartment. The petitioner testified that the apartment belonged to a friend who had given him a key to the apartment and allowed him to use it. On the day of his arrest, the petitioner testified that he let himself into the apartment. And on cross-examination, the petitioner stated that (1) he had a suit and shirt at the apartment, (2) he did not pay the owner for using the apartment, (3) he lived elsewhere, (4) the owner allowed him to use the apartment *as a friend*, and (5) on the night of the search and seizure the owner had been away from the apartment in another city for five days.

Based on this testimony, the federal district court denied petitioner's motion to suppress because the court concluded that the petitioner lacked standing (to object). The Court of Appeals affirmed the district court's decision denying the motion. Moreover, the Court of Appeals held that even if it had concluded that the petitioner had standing, it would have held that the evidence was lawfully admitted at trial.

On appeal, the Supreme Court determined that the issue of petitioner's stand ing was to be decided by referring to Rule 41(3) of the Federal Rules of Criminal Procedure. Although the Court noted that it was proper for the petitioner to establish that he was the victim of the government's invasion of his privacy, in order to challenge the legality of the search, it also recognized the petitioner's dilemma. Under the then-current law, if the petitioner sought to challenge the legality of a search he had to show that he had a possessory interest in the property searched. However, once he *admitted* that he possessed or had an interest in the premises, the prosecutor could later use his *admission* (from the pretrial proceeding) to convict him at trial. On the other hand, if the petitioner failed to assert an interest in the searched premises or the seized property, he was precluded from challenging the search, because he lacked *standing*. The Court rejected this state of the law.

The Court held in *Jones v. United States* that the petitioner had sufficiently established *standing* because (1) to hold otherwise would permit the government an advantage of contradictory positions as a basis for conviction (if *possession* is an essential element of the charge the government cannot deny that the defendant has standing to challenge the search), (2) the petitioner's testimony at the pretrial proceeding (motion to suppress) made out a sufficient interest in the premises to establish him as a person aggrieved by their search, and (3) he was legitimately on the premises where the search occurred. Accordingly, the Court held that a citizen-defendant had *automatic standing* to object to a Fourth Amendment violation if he could show that he was charged with a possessory offense or that he was legitimately on the premises. Nevertheless, in nonpossessory offenses a citizen-defendant continued to face the dilemma of making an incriminating statement in order to challenge (standing) a Fourth Amendment violation. The Court acknowledged that it had never considered squarely the question whether defendants charged with nonpossessory crimes are entitled to be relieved of this dilemma. Finally, the Court opined that it was *intolerable* for a citizen to give up his right to make a Fourth Amendment challenge in order to preserve his Fifth Amendment right against self-incrimination. Consequently, the Court held in *Simmons v. United States* that

> When a defendant testifies in support of a motion to suppress evidence on Fourth Amendment grounds, his testimony may not thereafter be admitted against him at trial on the issue of guilt unless he makes no objection.

Five years later in *Brown v. United States*, the Court was required to decide whether defendants who (1) were not on the premises at the time of the contested search and seizure; and (2) neither asserted ownership in the stolen goods found in the contested search of a third party's store nor (3) were charged with an offense that included possession of the stolen goods as an essential element, had standing to object. Although the *Brown* Court stated that it was not necessary to decide whether *Simmons v. United States* made *Jones v. United States automatic standing* unnecessary, it held that *automatic standing* did not apply to these facts.

> We simply see no reason to afford such automatic standing, where, as here, there was no risk to a defendant of either self-incrimination or prosecutorial self-contradiction.

Similarly, where the government violates the Fourth Amendment rights of a third party in order to secure evidence against a subsequently charged citizen, the Court has held that the citizen may not vicariously assert the rights of the searched (third party) person. In *Rakas v. Illinois*, the Court held that a person who is aggrieved by an illegal search and seizure only through the introduction of damaging evidence secured by a search of a third person's premises or property has not had any of his Fourth Amendment rights infringed. Nevertheless, the Court abandoned the concept of standing because it, in part, reaffirmed the principle that the rights assured by the Fourth Amendment are personal rights.

> But we think the better analysis forth-rightly focuses on the extent of a particular defendant's rights under the Fourth Amendment rather than on any theoretically separate, but invariably intertwined concept of standing.

Although property ownership did not necessarily give the owner a *personal right* to claim that his Fourth Amendment rights were violated, the Court had held that such ownership is *clearly a factor to be considered.* For example, in *Rawlings v. Kentucky*, the Court emphasized that ownership alone did not ensure a citizen's right to claim a Fourth Amendment violation. In *Rawlings*, the defendant asserted that he had a reasonable expectation of privacy in his female companion's purse, which supported his right to challenge the legality of searching that purse. That is, because he claimed ownership of the illegal drugs stored in his companion's purse, the defendant claimed that he should be entitled to challenge the search regardless of his expectation of privacy (in that purse). The Court disagreed with this contention:

> While petitioner's ownership of the drugs is undoubtedly one fact to be considered in this case, *Rakas* emphatically rejected the notion that arcane concepts of property law ought to control the ability to claim the protections of the Fourth Amendment.

The defendant's claim that he had a legitimate expectation of privacy in his companion's purse was undercut by several factors. First, the Court noted that he had never sought or received access to her purse prior to that sudden bailment. Second, the defendant did not have the right to exclude anyone else from his companion's purse. Third, and more important, the defendant made a frank admission during pretrial proceedings that he had no subjective expectation that Cox's (his companion) purse would remain free from governmental intrusion. In any event, ownership of the thing seized, or mere presence at the place searched, does not necessarily establish a legitimate expectation of privacy to challenge government action under the Fourth Amendment.

An Overnight Guest's *Expectation of Privacy* in His Host's Home

The Court has recognized that

> a person can have a legally sufficient interest in a place other than his own home so that the Fourth Amendment protects him from unreasonable governmental intrusion into that place.

Moreover, a person's capacity to claim the protection of the Fourth Amendment, the Court explained, does not depend on a property right but on whether that person had a legitimate expectation of privacy in the invaded place. However, one who merely claims to be *legitimately on the premises* may not claim the protection of the Fourth Amendment. On the other hand, a house guest may claim such an expectation of privacy in his host's premises. (Ricky Lyons, as an overnight guest, may claim an expectation of privacy in Steagald's premises).

In *Minnesota v. Olson*, a citizen was suspected of being an accomplice in a robbery-homicide at a gasoline station. Although the citizen-suspect was later arrested at his home, his accomplice could not be immediately found. With the assistance of a tip, the accomplice-defendant (defendant) was tracked to a duplex shared by a mother and her daughter. After confirming that the defendant was inside, the police surrounded the duplex. Without a warrant or consent, but with weapons drawn, the police entered the duplex and arrested the defendant. Less than an hour after his warrantless arrest, the defendant made an inculpatory statement. At a pretrial proceeding he moved to suppress this statement. The trial court denied defendant's motion to exclude the statement. The statement was admitted and the defendant was convicted. On appeal, the Minnesota Supreme Court held that the defendant had sufficient interests in his host's duplex to challenge the legality of the warrantless arrest. So the court reversed and ordered a new trial. The United States Supreme Court granted certiorari and affirmed.

The Supreme Court rejected the state's argument that the defendant could not have a legitimate expectation of privacy because he was never left alone in the duplex, nor was he given a key to the premises. According to the Court

> To hold that an overnight guest has a legitimate expectation of privacy in his host's home merely recognizes the every day expectations of privacy that we all share.

Furthermore, the Court observed that even though

> [t]he host may admit or exclude from the house as he prefers, [their guests] are entitled to a legitimate expectation of privacy despite the fact that they have no legal interest in the premises and do not have the legal authority to determine who may or may not enter the household.

This aspect of *Minnesota v. Olson* implies that *Rawlings v. Kentucky* may no longer be good law. That is, to enjoy an expectation of privacy in a third-party's premises, the social guest need not have the authority to exclude other guests. On the other hand, in *Minnesota v. Carter*, the Supreme Court had to decide whether defendants who occupied a consenting lessee's apartment for the sole purpose of bagging cocaine had a reasonable expectation of privacy in the apartment. Two members of the Court concluded that the defendants did not have a reasonable expectation of privacy in that apartment. These two justices reasoned that the facts of the case fell *somewhere in between* legitimately on the premises (no entitlement to Fourth Amendment protection) and the status of an overnight guest (entitled to protection). Because of the *purely commercial nature* of the defendants' activities in the apartment, the relatively short period of time on the premises, and the lack of any previous connection between the defendants and the lessee, these two justices concluded that the defendants were no more than *legitimately on the premises.* Nevertheless, these two justices also implied that someone other than an *overnight* guest may have an expectation of privacy in the host's home.

> There is no suggestion that they had a previous relationship with Thompson [host-lessee] or that there was any other purpose to their visit.

A concurring justice interpreted the Court's opinion to support the right of almost all social guests (overnight or not) to an expectation of privacy in the host's home.

> I join the Court's opinion, for its reasoning is consistent with my view that almost all social guests have a legitimate expectation of privacy, and hence protection against unreasonable searches, in the home.

According to the concurring justices, the defendants were merely legitimately on the premises. As a result, they had no reasonable expectation of privacy. One other concurring justice and the dissenters agreed that a social guest has a reasonable expectation of privacy in the host's home. So, a majority of the Court believes a social guest (not necessarily an overnight guest) may have a reasonable expectation of privacy in the host's home.

HYPOTHETICAL

Police Chief Marck Jackson (hereafter "Chief Jackson") of the Fayetteberg Police Department found the following anonymous letter under his office door around 7:30 am on May 29, 2004:

> I am an employee at Wal-Market Super Center on 12th Street in Fayetteberg. You should know that several people on the Wal-Market management staff at this store are selling powdered cocaine to kids at Fayetteberg High School and Romney Jr. High. Two kids at Romney Jr. High died from overdosing on this toxic dope. The street name of this cocaine is "Triple H."
>
> By the way, some of these Wal-Market managers are quite well-known in the community. Two of them are named "Bob." You know them well! They brag on how they've made so much money selling drugs and how they can hide it through their regular jobs. They sell the cocaine from the employee restrooms at the 12th Street store. They also use the employee lockers to store (and sometimes sell from) the drugs. The drugs are sometimes stored in their cars.

Chief Jackson conducted a search of police files to determine if any students from Romney Jr. High had recently died of toxic drugs. After a two-hour search he found records of three recent deaths by toxic drugs. Two of these deaths were of seventh graders at Canal Jr. High. The other death was of an eighth grader at Romney Jr. High. He also had several tips from reliable informants that "Bob" Sample sold drugs in the neighborhood.

After this search, Chief Jackson called the Wal-Market Home Office in Collierville. Chief Jackson identified himself and asked the appropriate personnel to locate the full name and address of the manager, "Jim Bob," at the 12th Street Super Center. After a ninety-minute search, the Home Office confirmed that there were two employee-managers at that store named "Bob." "Jim Bob" Sample was not only in his seventh year as a manager, but he was also a popular country-western singer in the Ozarks; and James Robert ("Bob") Powell was a two-year veteran and a popular thespian in a local theater troupe. "Bob" Powell, however, was on duty at a Wal-Market in China. So, Chief Jackson dispatched six officers to "Bob" Sample's home at 2342 Dayton Place. The officers were given a recent photograph of Sample so that they could identify him.

When the officers arrived at 2342 Dayton Place, they discovered that residence was enclosed on three sides by a five-foot wire mesh fence. The "open side" of the house was bordered by a driveway that extended in two directions. One direction led to an open carport at the back of the house. The alternate (left-side) direction led to an alley-way. On the other side of that alley-way was a residence with a cement shed located thirty feet away.

Officer Frank Pendleton took up an observation post across from 2342 Dayton Place. One hour after he took up this position Officer Pendleton saw a man drive up the open driveway of 2342 Dayton Place. As the man got out of the car Officer Pendleton recognized that the man was "Bob" Sample. He was wearing yellow gloves, and he was carrying a brown grocery bag in one hand. The officer observed that the grocery bag appeared to be "weighed-down" by its contents. Sample had a box of sandwich bags in his other hand. Officer Pendleton claims that, from his position, the powder on Sample's gloves appeared to be crack cocaine. At that moment, Officer Pendleton stepped into the street in front of the driveway and yelled at Sample, "Halt, Sample! This is the police. Freeze!"

Sample, according to Officer Pendleton, turned and looked at Officer Pendleton. However, he did not "freeze." Instead, Sample turned and walked away toward the left-branch direction of the driveway. Officer Pendleton and the other officers quickly pursued Sample down the alley. Sample walked across the alley-way to another property line where the cement shed was located. This property line boarded a single-family residence and backyard cement shed of his neighbor, Freda Clark. Clark's property was not enclosed; specifically, the border between her property line and the alley consisted of a fence, the cement shed, a four-foot opening, and a dilapidated three-foot fence.

Officer Pendleton saw Sample walk over to the shed, lift the corner of its tin roof, and drop the grocery bag into the shed. Pendleton then saw Sample discard his gloves and the box of baggies in a nearby trash can, which was also situated along the border of the Clark property adjacent to the alley-way. Sample turned and walked toward Pendleton and his fellow officers. Officer Pendleton handcuffed Sample and walked him to the police car. As they walked to the police car, Officer Pendleton asked Sample what he had thrown in the shed. Sample refused to answer.

After placing Sample in the back seat of a patrol car Officer Pendleton posted two officers at the patrol car to guard Sample. Then, Officer Pendleton walked back down the alley toward the cement shed on Clark's property. Accompanied by two other officers Officer Pendleton walked to the cement shed and attempted to lift its roof, but was unable to do so.

Meanwhile, Clark, the owner of both the residence and the cement shed, had already observed from her window that her neighbor, Sample, had been arrested and that a police officer was attempting to lift the roof of her cement shed. At that moment, a female officer knocked on Clark's door, and demanded that she step outside. Clark obeyed the officer's command. The female officer warned Clark that she would lose her home if she did not allow the officers to look inside the cement shed. Clark re-entered her house (with the female officer following close behind) and retrieved a key to the lock on the cement shed.

After Clark used the key to unlock the lock on the door to the shed, Pendleton and three other officers entered the shed. Officer Pendleton found the only grocery bag in that shed. He opened the grocery bag and found a scale and five separate bags each containing a substance that later field-tested positive for cocaine base. Officer Pendleton also recovered the yellow gloves and the baggies from the trash can. Sample was subsequently charged with intent to distribute more than one hundred grams of cocaine base.

Defendant Sample has lived across the alleyway from Clark and her family all of his life (twenty-eight years). So, the Clark and Sample families have been lifelong friends. Testimony at the suppression hearing will reveal that Clark's son, William "Buddy" Clark, and Sample were like brothers growing up. Each was an only child about the same age. Because their sons were like brothers the families often took vacations and threw parties together. Most people in the neighborhood thought the Clark-Sample families were one family.

Through the years, Sample would "live" over at the Clark house and "Buddy" would do the same at the Sample home. Although Clark had the only key to the cement shed she knew that "Buddy" and Sample used it as a "club house." She could look out her bedroom window and see the front of the shed thirty feet away. Because of her view she discovered that "Buddy" and Sample obtained access to the shed by lifting its tin roof and crawling inside. Clark never told her husband, or "Buddy" or Sample, that she knew they used the cement shed. She will testify that she was tempted to do so because she stored all her Christmas decorations in that shed and neither "Buddy" nor Sample had asked for permission to use it. Indeed, anyone (including her husband) seeking to use that shed had to ask for her permission to use, enter, or store anything in that shed. Clark will testify that neither her son nor Sample ever asked for permission to use the shed. However, she will testify that she had no objection to "family" sharing space in the shed. Besides, what was stored in those bags did not interfere with her privacy.

Clark will testify that after the young men turned twenty-one and began regular employment they did not use the shed very often. In the last five years she observed that they used the shed only two or three times a month. She will say that she saw them smoking "little" cigarettes, talking on their cell phones, drinking beer/wine, and storing paper boxes or bags of varying sizes and dimensions. However, she will deny that she knew Sample used the shed to store illegal drugs (cocaine).

Defendant is expected to file a motion to suppress contraband seized pursuant to a warrantless entry. You are an associate prosecutor. Please provide your senior prosecutor with a memorandum of law (1) analyzing the key legal precedents that the defendant will likely use to support his motions, (2) isolating the most persuasive arguments distilled from those precedents, and (3) predicting how the court is likely to rule on these competing arguments.

LIST OF READINGS

1. The Fourth Amendment to the United States Constitution.
2. Federal Rules of Evidence Rule 401. Definition of Relevant Evidence.
3. Federal Rules of Evidence Rule 402. Relevant Evidence Generally Admissible; Irrelevant Evidence Inadmissible.
4. *Mincey v. Arizona*, 437 U.S. 385 (1978).
5. *Watson v. United States*, 423 U.S. 11 (1976).
6. *Katz v. United States*, 389 U.S. 347 (1967).
7. *Carroll v. United States*, 267 U.S. 132 (1925).
8. *Atwater v. City of Lago Vista*, 532 U.S. 318 (2001).
9. *Whren v. United States*, 517 U.S. 806 (1996).
10. *Wilson v. Arkansas*, 514 U.S. 927 (1995).
11. *Welsh v. Wisconsin*, 466 U.S. 740 (1995).
12. *Virginia v. Moore*, 533 U.S. 164 (2008).
13. *Wong Sun v. United States*, 371 U.S. 471 (1963).

14. *United States v. Robinson*, 414 U.S. 218 (1973).
15. *Knowles v. Iowa*, 525 U.S. 113 (1998).
16. *Ker v. California*, 374 U.S. 23 (1963).
17. *Gerstein v. Pugh*, 420 U.S. 103 (1975).
18. *County of Riverside v. McLaughlin*, 500 U.S. 44 (1991).
19. *McNabb v. United States*, 318 U.S. 332 (1943).
20. *Mallory v. United States*, 354 U.S. 449 (1957).
21. *Coolidge v. New Hampshire*, 403 U.S. 443 (1971).
22. *Payton v. New York*, 445 U.S. 573 (1980).
23. *Mapp v. Ohio*, 367 U.S. 643 (1961).
24. *Steagald v. United States*, 451 U.S. 204 (1981).
25. *Rakas v. Illinois*, 439 U.S. 128 (1978).
26. *Minnesota v. Olson*, 495 U.S. 91 (1990).
27. *Boyd v. United States*, 116 U.S. 616 (1886).
28. *Jones v. United States*, 362 U.S. 257 (1960).
29. *Brown v. United States*, 411 U.S. 223 (1973).
30. *Alderman v. United States*, 394 U.S. 165 (1969).
31. *Rakas v. Illinois*, 439 U.S. 128 (1978).
32. *United States v. Salvucci*, 448 U.S. 83 (1980).
33. *Minnesota v. Carter*, 525 U.S. 83 (1998).

SAMPLE ESSAY

To: Senior Prosecutor
From: Associate Prosecutor
Re: Pretrial Proceedings, Defendant's Motion-to-suppress contraband seized pursuant to a warrantless entry
Date:

In anticipation of the upcoming *motion-in-limine* by the defendant identified above, I have prepared the following memorandum explaining the issues involved and our possible response to them. Essentially the defendant will argue that Officer Pendleton entered the cement shed without a warrant or other lawful justification. As a result, he will claim that the cocaine found in the cement shed should be excluded as fruits of an unlawful entry. We can, however, show in response, that Sample had no expectation of privacy in his neighbor's cement shed. *Rakas v. Illinois*, 439 U.S. 128 (1978).

As our response asserts that the defendant is precluded from challenging a Fourth Amendment violation because he was not the person aggrieved by an unlawful search or seizure, it is the defendant's burden to show the trial court that as the proponent seeking exclusion he has alleged an injury in fact to his own Fourth Amendment rights. Hence, the trial court must determine whether the disputed search or seizure has violated an interest of the defendant that the Fourth Amendment was designed to protect. Even if the trial court determines that someone's (other than the defendant's) Fourth Amendment rights were violated, the defendant could not invoke the exclusionary rule to vindicate a Fourth Amendment violation to another person. So, the cocaine will be admitted because the defendant is precluded by law from asserting a challenge. In any event, my analysis of how we should prevail in this matter is set out below.

PART A. THE GENERAL RULE OF ADMISSIBILITY

Federal Rule of Evidence 401 provides that all relevant evidence is admissible except as *otherwise* provided by the Constitution of the United States. Because the Fourth Amendment to the United States Constitution prohibits unreasonable searches and seizures, any unreasonable search or seizure violates the Fourth Amendment. For example, the Supreme Court has held that a warrantless search of a citizen's telephone conversation by an agent of the government violates the Fourth Amendment. *Katz v. United States*, 389 U.S. 347 (1967). More important, in order to ensure the effectiveness of this Fourth Amendment protection, the Supreme Court has held that evidence seized as a result of the unlawful search could not constitute proof at trial against the victim of the search.

At the pretrial proceedings the judge must determine whether the disputed search or seizure has violated an interest of the defendant that the Fourth Amendment was designed to protect. An analysis of the law applied to our facts follows.

PART B. THE RIGHT TO CHALLENGE A FOURTH AMENDMENT VIOLATION

At the suppression hearing we should expect the defendant-Sample to contend that the Fourth Amendment protects him against unreasonable searches and seizures. Here he will claim that the police violated his Fourth Amendment rights by entering the cement shed without a warrant. He will then argue that the court should exclude the cocaine found in the grocery bag from his trial because it is the fruit of that warrantless entry. Furthermore the defendant will contend that the admissibility of the cocaine should turn on whether Officer Pendleton's warrantless entry into the cement shed was an unreasonable search under the Fourth Amendment. However, we will argue that the applicable law precludes the defendant from asserting a Fourth Amendment violation because his rights under the Fourth Amendment were not violated.

The heart of defendant-Sample's argument will be based, in part, on language and reasoning from three United States Supreme Court opinions: *Rakas v. Illinois*, *Minnesota v. Olson*, and *Minnesota v. Carter*. Whether examined individually or collectively neither opinion appears to support the defendant's claim that he had an expectation of privacy in Clark's cement shed.

Rakas

Among other things, *Rakas* held that the capacity to claim the protection of the Fourth Amendment, thus the right to challenge a search or seizure, requires a citizen to show that he had a legitimate expectation of privacy in the invaded place. Moreover, the *Rakas* Court held that a citizen may have a legally sufficient interest in a place other than his own home. Even so, Sample is required to make a showing that he had a legitimate expectation of privacy in Clark's cement shed. Such a showing must be supported by either *Olson* or *Carter*.

Olson

Olson merely held that an overnight guest's expectation of privacy was legitimate and protected by the Fourth Amendment because such an expectation is rooted in understandings that are recognized and permitted by society. However, at the time

Officer Pendleton searched Clark's cement shed, Sample was neither an overnight guest of the Clark's house nor of her shed. Even *Rakas* would preclude an overnight guest of the Clark house from claiming an expectation of privacy in the Clarks' cement shed. Consequently, Sample's claim of an expectation of privacy in Clark's shed is not supported by either *Rakas* or *Olson. Minnesota v. Carter* is the defendant's final option.

Carter

In *Carter* the Court observed that an overnight guest may claim the protection of the Fourth Amendment while a guest in his host's home, but that a guest who was merely legitimately on the premises could not. Two members of the *Carter* plurality stated that a guest who was present at his host's home for essentially a business transaction, such as bagging cocaine, and where he was only present in the home for a few hours, was not entitled to Fourth Amendment protection. On the other hand, these same two justices implied that a guest may claim Fourth Amendment protection if he either had (1) a previous relationship with the host-owner, (2) any other purpose to his visit, or (3) an overnight guest relationship as in *Minnesota v. Olson*.

Two other members of the Court who reluctantly concurred accepted the principle that an overnight guest could claim Fourth Amendment protection. However, these two members would not accept the principle that a guest who was something less than an overnight guest could claim the right to Fourth Amendment protection. The remaining members of the Court appear to accept that a guest other than an overnight guest may claim Fourth Amendment protection.

Unlike Clark's relationship with Sample in our facts, the host in *Minnesota v. Carter* had received the defendants into her apartment as guests in exchange for a small quantity of cocaine. As a consequence, we should argue, Sample was neither a guest nor an invitee. Indeed, he was not legitimately on the premises. Accordingly he had no reasonable expectation of privacy in the premises.

There is some weight to the defendant's response to our arguments; that is, the defendant may correctly contend that *Carter* permits a court to consider not only the commercial use of the property, but the prior relationship between Sample and his host, Clark. Coupling these *Carter* factors with other known facts in this hypothetical may support Sample's claim that he had a legitimate expectation of privacy in Clark's cement shed. The Court may conclude that Sample has the right to challenge the warrantless search of Clark's cement shed because (1) they share a significant family relationship; (2) Sample used the shed for noncommercial purposes; (3) Sample has used the shed for commercial and noncommercial purposes for the past five years; (4) Clark knew Sample entered the shed by a route and method other than through the locked door, but that she did not object; and (5) Clark knew that he used the shed but she did not object to its use.

TOOLS FOR SELF-CRITICISM

The determination whether Sample has an expectation of privacy in Clark's cement shed is primarily controlled by *Minnesota v. Carter*. As discussed above in *Carter* a citizen has no expectation of privacy in a third-party's premises if he is neither an overnight guest, a person with a previous relationship with the host-owner, a person whose visit was for a purpose other than a commercial one, or a person who had an overnight guest relationship as in *Minnesota v. Olson*, that is a relationship that would suggest a degree of acceptance into the household. As the Court has not defined the scope of previous relationship with the host-owner, courts must conduct a fact-specific case analysis to determine this issue. Hence, a twenty-eight-year-old relationship of being treated as a member of Clark's family, and vice versa, may qualify.

If there is no previous relationship between Clark and Sample, then the fact that the shed was used solely to conceal illegal drugs will eliminate a defendant's standing to challenge the constitutionality of the search.

VARIATIONS ON A THEME

Try the same problem, but this time the Clark and the Sample families do not know each other, and Clark thought she was the only one using the shed. Does this change the result?

SEARCH INCIDENT TO AN ARREST OR A STOP

7

OPENING REMARKS

The United States Supreme Court has held that a search incident to a lawful arrest involves two types of warrantless searches: the arrestee's person and the area within his immediate control. However, unlike the Court's long stretch of constantly shifting interpretations of what constitutes the area within an arrestee's immediate control, its opinions on the search of the arrestee's person have been relatively static for a century. Since its seminal opinion in *Weeks v. United States* the Court has repeatedly affirmed the broadly stated rule that an arresting officer may automatically search an arrestee's person. The Court has specifically delineated the scope of the police authority to conduct a search of the person after a lawful arrest.

Search of the Person

In *United States v. Robinson,* the United States Supreme Court determined that the justification or reason for the police authority to conduct a search of the arrestee's person after a lawful arrest rests as much on the need to disarm the suspect, in order to take him into custody, as it does on the need to preserve evidence on his person for later use at trial. The Court emphasized that disarming an arrestee is critically important because the officer is in far greater danger due to his extended exposure that follows his taking the suspect into custody and then transporting him to jail. The Court concluded that a custodial arrest based on probable cause is a reasonable intrusion under the Fourth Amendment. And as the arrest was lawful, a search of the person incident to that lawful arrest requires no additional justification. Consequently, the Court opined that a full search of the person (and any containers on his person) is always reasonable as an incident to a lawful custodial arrest. Moreover, the Court has held that this reasonable search of the person was not dependent on the existence of police department policy establishing the conditions under which a full-scale body search should be conducted.

Search of the Person at the Jail Facility

In *Maryland v. King*, the Court held that neither probable cause nor any other prior justification is required to justify the police intrusion into a citizen's mouth to perform a cheek swab in order to obtain a recent detainee's DNA sample; the Court reasoned that a buccal swab involved a brief and minimal intrusion with "virtually no risk, trauma, or pain."

The Court (*Florence v. Board of Chosen Freeholders*) has rejected a citizen's 42 U.S.C. § 1983 civil action against government entities (jailers) for allegedly violating his Fourth and Fourteenth Amendment rights. The citizen-detainee claimed that because he was arrested for only a minor offense, he could not be subjected to an invasive search (stop search) at the jail unless the jail officials had reason to suspect that he was concealing weapons, drugs, or other contraband. Such search procedures, argued the Court, in jail facilities should be left to the expertise of correctional officials who are charged with maintaining safety and order in detention centers. The Court reasoned that a regulation impinging on an inmate's constitutional rights must be upheld "if it is reasonably related to legitimate penological interests." Moreover, the Court concluded that the search procedures employed struck a reasonable balance between the inmate's privacy interests and the needs of the jail facility.

Search of the Area within the Suspect's Immediate Control or the Area Where He Was Arrested

As early as 1925, the Court recognized the right of an arresting officer to search the person of the arrestee and the area in the arrestee's control at the time of that arrest, *Agnello v. United States*. Although the Court explicitly recognized that an arresting officer had the right to search, without a warrant, an arrestee's person and the area in his immediate control, it had difficulty defining the scope of the area within that control. Initially the Court held that the police may not conduct a warrantless search of an arrestee's home merely because he was lawfully arrested several blocks away in a third-party's home. Hence, a warrantless search of an arrestee's house is not incident to a lawful arrest, blocks away, in the home of a third party. However, even when the lawful arrest and the search incident to that arrest occurred in the same place, the Court still struggled to define the scope of a lawful search incident to an arrest.

From 1927 to 1964, the Court vacillated on whether it was constitutional for the police to conduct a warrantless search in the place where the arrest occurred. The Court concluded in *Chimel v. California* that a more precise method of analysis was required in this area of search incident to a lawful arrest. In *Chimel*, the Court held that it is reasonable for an arresting officer to search the person of an arrestee in order to remove any weapons that the latter might seek to use in order to resist arrest or effect his escape, or to prevent him from concealing or destroying evidence. Similarly, concluded the Court, the area into which an arrestee might reach in order to grab a weapon or evidentiary items must, of course, be governed by a like rule. The Court defined the area within the arrestee's immediate control to mean the area from which he might gain possession of a weapon or destructible evidence.

So, according to *Chimel* the facts and circumstances of each case must be considered in order to determine whether there is ample justification for a search of the area within the arrestee's immediate control. The Court opined that there could be no comparable justification for routinely searching any room, even the one in which an arrest occurs. Moreover, the Court found no justification for searching through all the desk drawers or other closed or concealed areas in the room where the arrest is made, unless such a search is made pursuant to a warrant or a recognized exception to a warrant. Likewise, a search of the house where the arrest occurred is not reasonable unless it is made pursuant to an exception to the warrant requirement—a *protective sweep* is covered more fully, later in this chapter, under *Terry v. Ohio* and its progeny.

Search of a Suspect's Car—Incident to an Arrest

After *Chimel*, the Court acknowledged that though the principle that limits a search incident to a lawful arrest may be stated clearly enough, it was not universally applicable. For example, despite this clarity the Court noted that lower courts have had difficulty applying this straightforward rule to the narrow class of cases concerning whether in the course of a search incident to a lawful custodial arrest of occupants of an automobile the police may search the interior of that automobile if the arrestees are no longer inside. The Court considered this lack of clarity unacceptable because it prevented a citizen from knowing the scope of his constitutional protection, and it prevented the police officer from knowing the scope of her authority. The Court sought to resolve this matter in *New York v. Belton.*

The *Belton* Court held that when a police officer has made a lawful custodial arrest of the occupant of an automobile, he may, as a contemporaneous incident of that arrest, search the passenger compartment of that automobile (but not the trunk). Based on its holding and the reasons supporting it, the *Belton* Court concluded that the police may also examine the contents of a container found in the passenger compartment of that car during the search incident to this lawful arrest. That is, the search of a container found in the passenger compartment was lawful whether the container was open or closed. The *Belton* Court read *United States v. Robinson* (search of the *person*) to permit the arresting police officers to search a closed container even if it could not hold a weapon or evidence of criminal conduct.

Approximately twenty-four years after *Belton,* the Court was requested to determine in *Thornton v. United States* whether *Belton* was limited to a situation where the policeman initiated contact with the arrestee while the arrestee was still an occupant of the car. On the whole, *Thornton* appears to reject any such limitation on *Belton.* In *Thornton*, the Supreme Court held that *Belton* allows the police to search the passenger compartment of a vehicle incident to a lawful arrest of both occupants and recent occupants.

The Court revisited *Belton* and *Thornton* in *Arizona v. Gant.* Gant was arrested pursuant to an outstanding warrant for his arrest for driving with a suspended license. He was handcuffed about twelve feet away from his closed car. After he was placed in the police car, the arresting officer conducted a warrantless search of Gant's car. During that search, the police found a gun and a bag of cocaine in the pocket of a jacket on the back seat. Gant moved to suppress these items seized from his car, on the grounds that the warrantless search violated the Fourth Amendment. The Court held that the search was lawful under *Belton* only when an arrestee is unsecured and within reaching distance of the passenger compartment of the car at the time of the search. Gant was secured (handcuffed and in the back seat of a locked police car). The *Gant* Court acknowledged that the *Belton* opinion had been widely understood to allow a vehicle search incident to the arrest of a recent occupant even if there is no possibility that the arrestee could gain access to the vehicle at the time of the search. The Court rejected this broad reading of *Belton.* Although Justice Scalia concurred in *Gant*, he rejected the notion that *Chimel* applied to this set of facts.

Additionally, the *Gant* Court held that because of the circumstances unique to the vehicle context a warrantless search incident to a lawful arrest is justified (even if the citizen is secured in the police car) when it is reasonable for the police officer to believe evidence relevant to the crime might be found in the vehicle. Gant wins under this principle as well because he was arrested for an offense (driving with a suspended license) where the police officer could not reasonably believe evidence relevant to the crime might be found in the vehicle. If the officer had such a reasonable belief based on the nature of the offense, he would be allowed to search the passenger compartment and any containers within it. On the other hand, the Court has held that none of these rationales supporting a search incident to a lawful arrest apply to a search incident to a citation (fine-only crime).

Search Incident to Something Less than a Custodial Arrest

The Fourth Amendment is implicated when a government agent conducts a search or seizure. A search or seizure is presumptively reasonable if it was made pursuant to a warrant or a recognized exception to a warrant. A search incident to a lawful custodial arrest is a recognized exception to the warrant requirement. And, a search incident to a lawful custodial arrest allows the arresting officer to conduct a warrantless search of the arrestee's person and the area within his immediate control. Moreover, the police may conduct a warrantless search of a person incident to a seizure other than a custodial arrest, and based on fewer facts than required to establish probable cause. Hence, in order to appreciate a search incident to a seizure that is less intrusive than a custodial arrest, and that is based on fewer facts than the probable cause requirement, an examination of *Terry v. Ohio* is necessary.

Based on almost forty years of police experience, a plainclothes police detective suspected three men (one of the three was Terry) of preparing to rob a store. Upon approaching the three men to dispel his suspicion, the detective seized them and searched their outer clothing, and discovered that two of the three men possessed guns. The defendants argued that the guns should be suppressed as fruits of a Fourth Amendment violation. The trial court denied these motions because it felt that not only had the detective acted reasonably by conducting a pat-down of the suspects' outer clothing (because he believed they were armed), but that such a pat-down of a citizen's outer clothing was outside the protection of the Fourth Amendment.

Under these facts, the Court opined that there could be no question that the detective seized Terry and subjected him to a search when he took hold of him and patted down the outer surfaces of his clothing. Accordingly, the Court had to decide whether it was reasonable for the detective to have interfered with Terry's personal security as he did.

> And in determining whether the seizure and search were "unreasonable" our inquiry is a dual one… whether the officer's action was justified at its inception, and whether it was reasonably related in scope to the circumstances which justified the interference in the first place.

In *Terry*, the Court emphatically rejected the notion that this conduct of the police described as a stop and frisk was outside the purview of the Fourth Amendment, or that neither action rose to the level of a search or seizure within the meaning of the Constitution. According to the *Terry* Court, it was simply fantastic to contend that placing a citizen with his hands raised while being groped by the police constituted only a petty indignity. The Court considered this frisk a serious intrusion upon the sanctity of the person, and something not to be undertaken lightly.

In *Terry*, the Court devised the following test for determining the reasonableness of police action under this stop-and-frisk rubric of police conduct. The Court said there is no ready test for determining reasonableness other than by balancing the need to search or seize against the invasion that the search or seizure entails.

In order to justify an intrusion on a citizen's Fourth Amendment interests on a less-than-probable-cause basis a police officer must be able to point to specific and articulable facts that, taken together with rational inferences from those facts, reasonably warrant that intrusion. Moreover, the state must show that those facts known by the officer at the moment of the seizure or search would warrant a man of reasonable caution in the belief that the action taken was appropriate. Although the *Terry* Court spoke of a search or a seizure, it clearly did not decide anything about the constitutional propriety of an investigative seizure (stop and interrogate) upon less-than-probable cause. A *Terry* stop and interrogate is covered later in this chapter under in the section "Stop and Interrogate on Less-than-Probable Cause."

Terry's Progeny

Whether it is called a search or seizure pursuant to probable cause or a stop and frisk based on something less than probable cause, the *Terry* Court recognized that the Fourth Amendment governs all intrusions by agents of the government upon a citizen's personal security. Therefore in order to assess the reasonableness of an officer's invasion of a citizen's personal security on a less-than-probable-cause basis, a court must consider three factors. First, a court must consider the governmental interest justifying the intrusion. That is, the police officer must be able to point to specific and articulable facts that taken together with rational inferences (from those facts) reasonably warrant that intrusion.

Second, a judge must *balance* that need to search or seize against the invasion that the search (or seizure) entails. To complete this reasonableness assessment, a court must, third, evaluate all the facts against an objective standard.

In other words, did the police officer observe unusual conduct that led him to reasonably conclude in light of his experience that criminal activity may be afoot, and that the persons with whom he is dealing may be armed and presently dangerous? The Supreme Court in *Sibron v. New York* identified the requirements for a frisk:

> The police officer is not entitled to seize and search every person whom he sees on the street or of whom he makes inquiries. Before he places a hand on the person of a citizen in search of anything, he must have constitutionally adequate, reasonable grounds for doing so. In the case of the self-protective search for weapons, he must be able to point to particular facts from which he reasonably inferred that the individual was armed and dangerous.

Hence, concluded the Court, a suspect's mere act of talking with a number of known narcotics addicts over an eight-hour period did not justify a reasonable belief by the police that they were in danger, nor did it support probable cause to arrest. Reasonable suspicion, the Court has determined, is *somewhat abstract*. That is, the Court has deliberately avoided reducing it (reasonable suspicion) to a neat set of legal rules. It is, however, clear that the Court adopts the *totality of the circumstances* test as the governing principle for determining the existence *vel non* of reasonable suspicion.

The Court has held that a law enforcement agent may stop a citizen on facts that amount to less than probable cause to arrest if the officer can point to specific and articulable facts that, taken together with rational inferences from those facts, would warrant a man of reasonable caution in the belief that a brief investigative stop is appropriate. Consistent with this stop the officer may take steps to assure himself that the person with whom he is dealing is not armed with a weapon that could unexpectedly and fatally be used against him. And when conducting that pat-down if the officer feels what he immediately recognizes as contraband (non-weapon), he may reach inside the clothing and seize it pursuant to the plain feel doctrine (*Minnesota v. Dickerson*). However, *Minnesota v. Dickerson* specifically held that the plain feel exception will not apply even if the initial stop is lawful under *Terry v. Ohio*, but in order to determine that the lump is contraband, the officer must squeeze, slide, and otherwise manipulate the contents of the suspect's pocket.

Specific and articulable facts supporting reasonable suspicion to stop and frisk have covered a wide spectrum of circumstances. In *Illinois v. Wardlow* the Court held that a citizen's headlong flight from a high crime area resulted in a common-sense judgment that the officer possessed reasonable suspicion to lawfully stop and frisk. Although the Court has noted that a citizen's presence in an area of expected criminal activity, standing alone, is not enough to support a reasonable particularized suspicion that the person is committing a crime, the fact that the stop occurred in a high crime area is among the relevant contextual considerations in a *Terry* analysis.

Reasonable Suspicion to Search for Weapons in an Automobile Passenger Compartment—*Terry* Search of a Car

In *Michigan v. Long* the Court held that the search of an automobile's passenger compartment was reasonable under *Terry v. Ohio*

> "if the police officer possesses a reasonable belief based on 'specific and articulable facts, which taken together with the rational inferences from those facts, reasonably warrant' the officer in believing that the suspect is dangerous and the suspect may gain immediate control of the weapons."

Reasonable Suspicion Based on an Informant's Tip

Specific language in *Terry* suggests that an officer's reasonable suspicion to stop and frisk may only occur when the officer has personally observed the suspicious conduct.

> That is, the Court said, but we deal with an entire rubric of police conduct… necessarily swift action predicated upon the on-the-spot observations of the officer on the beat…

Despite *Terry*'s language, however, the Court has held that a police officer may develop reasonable suspicion to stop and frisk based on facts supplied by an informant. For example, in *Adams v. Williams* the Court held that after a police officer was told by a known informant that a suspect sitting in a nearby car had a gun at his waist, the officer man did not act unreasonably by approaching that car, tapping on the driver's window, and asking the driver to open the door. When the driver rolled down the window instead, the Court held that is was not unreasonable for the officer to reach in the suspect's waist and remove the gun.

Similarly, in *Alabama v. White* the Court held that a corroborated tip from an anonymous informant supported a reasonable suspicion to stop and frisk. In *White*, the police received an anonymous tip (1) asserting that a woman would be carrying cocaine from a particular location, and (2) predicting that this woman would leave a particular apartment building at a certain time, get into a car matching a specific description, and drive to a particular motel. The Court conceded that an anonymous tip alone seldom demonstrates the informant's basis of knowledge or veracity (*Aguilar/Spinelli* test under Chapter 2) sufficient enough to support reasonable suspicion. Nevertheless,

> The Court held that although it was a close case, it concluded that under a totality of the circumstances the anonymous tip, as corroborated, exhibited sufficient indicia of reliability to justify, the investigatory stop of respondent's car.

On the other hand, the Court has held in *Florida v. J.L.* that a police officer did not have *reasonable suspicion* to stop and frisk when his actions were based on information from an uncorroborated anonymous tip. This tip, according to the Court, lacked the moderate indicia of reliability present in *White* that was essential to the Court's decision in that case. According to the Court, this anonymous tip did not contain any predictive information upon which the police could corroborate or otherwise test this information.

A Search beyond an Arrestee's Immediate Area of Control, Protective Sweep Based on Suspicion Pursuant to *Terry*

In *Maryland v. Buie*, the Court examined circumstances that expanded the reach of a search incident to a lawful arrest.

The Court noted that the Fourth Amendment bars only unreasonable searches and seizures. In determining reasonableness the Court balances the intrusion of the individual's Fourth Amendment interests against the promotion of legitimate governmental interests. Like the protective pat-down in *Terry* and *Long* a protective sweep of a house could provide a similar protective assurance. The Court requires articulable facts that taken with the rational inferences from those facts would warrant a reasonably prudent officer in believing that the areas to be swept harbors an individual posing a danger to those on the arrest scene.

The Court identified an analogous interest of the officers in taking steps to assure themselves that the house in which a suspect is being arrested is not harboring other persons who might attack them. Like the protective pat-down in *Terry* and *Long*, a protective sweep of a house could provide such assurance.

> The *Buie* Court held that there must be articulable facts which, taken together with the rational inferences from those facts, would warrant a reasonably prudent officer in believing that the areas to be swept harbors an individual posing a danger to those on the arrest scene.

Unfortunately, the *Buie* Court did not limit itself to this one holding.

> The Court also held that as an incident to the arrest the officers could, as a precautionary matter and without probable cause or reasonable suspicion, look in

> closets and other spaces, immediately adjoining the place of arrest from which an attack could be immediately launched.

This is an unfortunate holding because the *Buie* Court only had to decide what level of justification is required by the Fourth and Fourteenth Amendments before police officers may conduct a warrantless protective sweep of all or part of the premises. Although the Court determined that the level of justification for a protective sweep was less than a probable cause requirement, its precautionary matter holding does not require probable cause or reasonable suspicion. How could the certified question require a level of justification, but the uncertified query require no level of justification? Perhaps the Court intended to limit this additional holding to the specific facts in *Buie* where the arrestee's accomplice is unaccounted for at the time of the arrest. The Court, however, does not explain.

Stop and Interrogate on Less than Probable Cause

The *Terry* Court specifically cautioned that it did not decide anything about the constitutional propriety of an investigative seizure (stop and interrogate), upon less than probable cause. However, thirty-six years after the *Terry* decision the Court in *Hiibel v. Sixth Judicial District Court* held that a police officer may seize, detain, and question (interrogate) a citizen on less than probable cause.

Hiibel was lawfully stopped (*Terry*) by a deputy sheriff who explained that he was investigating a report of a fight. When asked if he had any identification, Hiibel demanded to know why he had to produce it. Although the deputy threatened to arrest Hiibel if he did not produce some identification, the Hiibel refused to do so.

Hiibel was charged with willfully resisting, delaying, or obstructing a public officer in discharging or attempting to discharge a legal duty of his office in violation of applicable Nevada law. This state law required, in part, that a person who has been detained by a peace officer, under circumstances which reasonably indicate that the detained person has committed a crime, shall identify himself. Hiibel argued that this state law violated the Fourth and Fifth Amendments.

Generally, Hiibel argued that his conviction could not stand because the officer's conduct violated the Fourth Amendment. Specifically, Hiibel claimed that *Terry v. Ohio* provided that a citizen could not be arrested and prosecuted for refusing to answer an officer's questions during a lawful *Terry* stop. Because of precise language in the *Terry* opinion, Hiibel claimed the deputy violated Hiibel's Fourth Amendment rights by arresting him for refusing to identify himself.

> In *Terry*, Justice White stated in a concurring opinion, that a person detained in an investigative stop can be questioned but is not obliged to answer, answers may not be compelled and refusal to answer furnishes no basis for an arrest.

The Court rejected the argument and the quote from *Terry* supporting it.

> We do not read these statements as controlling. The passages recognize that the Fourth Amendment does not impose obligations on the citizen, but instead provide rights against the government. As a result, the Fourth Amendment itself can not

> require a suspect to answer questions. This case concerns a different issue, however. Here the source of the legal obligation arises from Nevada State law, not the Fourth Amendment.

Hence, the Court concluded that the particular language in Justice White's concurrence did not answer the question of whether a state can compel a suspect to disclose his name during a *Terry* stop. As long as a *Terry* stop is justified at its inception (based on articulable facts), a question requesting identification that is reasonably related in scope to the circumstances that justified the stop will be considered constitutional.

Consensual Encounter or a Fourth Amendment Seizure

The United States Supreme Court has held that the Fourth Amendment is *implicated* when the government conducts a search or seizure. A *seizure*, the Court has determined, may involve a custodial arrest, a stop and frisk, a stop and interrogate (including a traffic stop), or a situation when either a police officer uses physical force to detain a person or a person submits or yields to a police officer's show of authority. On the other hand, consensual *encounters* or those unrelated to the detection and investigation of criminal conduct do not implicate the Fourth Amendment: for example, when police are engaged in so-called *community care taking* tasks (i.e., removing abandoned cars from the highway).

The Court has held that a person is seized by the police and thus entitled to challenge the government's action under the Fourth Amendment when the government's action, by means of physical force or show of authority, terminates or restrains the person's freedom of movement through means *intentionally applied.* Generally the Court has determined that a seizure does not occur simply because a police officer approaches an individual and asks a few questions (this is a *consensual* encounter), so long as a reasonable person would feel free to disregard the police and go about his business. Indeed, no justification is required for the police to approach (consensually encounter) a citizen under such circumstances. The Court has held in *Florida v. Bostick* that a police officer's act of *approaching* a person and asking a few questions is merely a consensual encounter, and reasonable suspicion is not required to justify it. Accordingly, the Court has devised a test for determining when a police–citizen *encounter* becomes a *seizure* (or is no longer consensual). This test was created by the Court combining holdings from two apparent conflicting opinions: *United States v. Mendenhall* and *California v. Hodari D.*

From 1980 to 1991, the Court's test for determining whether a police–citizen *encounter* constituted a *seizure* was derived from *United States v. Mendenhall.* Although the Court's reasons for holding the agents' actions constitutional were fractured between a no-seizure theory and a reasonable-seizure basis, a singular test for determining a Fourth Amendment seizure emerged from *Mendenhall.*

> We conclude that a person has been "seized" within the meaning of the Fourth Amendment only if, in view of all the circumstances surrounding the incident, a reasonable person would have believed that he was not free to leave.

This holding appeared at once to be both emphatic and dispositive about how *seizure* would be determined. However, in 1991 the Court held that satisfying

Mendenhall's free to leave test would not alone, determine whether a seizure has occurred under the Fourth Amendment.

In *California v. Hodari D* the Court rejected a respondent's reliance on the language in *Mendenhall* that provided that a person has been seized within the meaning of the Fourth Amendment only if a reasonable person would have believed that he was not free to leave. *Hodari D* held that a seizure only occurs where either the police brings the citizen under control or the citizen submits to the police assertion of authority.

On the other hand, this free-to-leave *necessary* step for determining a seizure is inappropriate when determining whether an employee at his worksite or a passenger on a bus had been seized under the Fourth Amendment. Because as the Court explained it

> [w]hen the person is seated on a bus he has no desire to leave, the degree to which a reasonable person would feel that he or she could leave is not an accurate measure of the coercive effect of the encounter.

Instead, where the police activity did not confine either the employee to his worksite or the passenger to the bus a different test for determining seizure has been established by the Court.

> In *Florida v. Bostick*, the Court stated that it adhered to the rule that in order to determine whether a particular encounter constitutes a seizure, a court must consider all the circumstances surrounding the encounter to determine whether the police conduct would have communicated to a reasonable person that the person was not free to decline the officers' requests or otherwise terminate the encounter.

This rule, the Court added, applies to encounters that take place on a city street as well as on a bus. The Court also rejected the argument that a citizen must have been seized because no reasonable person would freely consent to a search of luggage that he knows contains drugs. This argument cannot prevail, opined the Court, because the reasonable person test presupposes an *innocent* person.

HYPOTHETICAL

Police Chief Marck Jackson (hereafter "Chief Jackson") of the Fayetteberg Police Department found the following anonymous letter under his office door around 7:30 am on May 29,2004:

> I am an employee at Wal-Market Super Center on 12th Street in Fayetteberg. You should know that several people on the Wal-Market management staff at this store are selling powdered cocaine to kids at Fayetteberg High School and Romney Jr. High. Two kids at Romney Jr. High died from overdosing on this toxic dope. The street name of this cocaine is "Triple H."
>
> By the way, some of these Wal-Market managers are quite well-known in the community. Two of them are named "Bob." You know them well! They brag on how they've made so much money selling drugs and how they can hide it through their regular jobs. They sell the cocaine from the employee restrooms at the 12th

Street store. Sometimes Bob sells drugs from a black jeep. When he sells from that jeep he is usually accompanied by a very young blond woman. The woman usually carries the drugs and money for him. They also use the employee lockers to store (and sometimes sell from) the drugs. The drugs are sometimes stored in their cars.

Chief Jackson conducted a search of police files to determine if any students from Romney Jr. High had recently died of toxic drugs. After a two-hour search he found records of three recent deaths by toxic drugs. Two of these deaths were of seventh graders at Canal Jr. High. The other death was of an eighth grader at Romney Jr. High. He also had several tips from reliable informants that "Bob" Sample sold drugs in the neighborhood.

After this search, Chief Jackson called the Wal-Market Home Office in Collierville. Chief Jackson identified himself and asked the appropriate personnel to locate the full name and address of the manager, "Jim Bob," at the 12th Street Super Center. After a ninety-minute search, the Home Office confirmed that there were two employee-managers at that store named, "Bob." "Jim Bob" Sample was not only in his seventh year as a manager, but he was also a popular country-western singer in the Ozarks. Chief Jackson found hundreds of photographs depicting Bob Sample in advertisements for country-and-western shows throughout the Ozarks. James Robert ("Bob") Powell was a two-year veteran and a popular thespian in a local theater troupe. "Bob" Powell, however, was on duty at a Wal-Market in China.

Chief Jackson sent a team of six officers, led by Officer Frank Pendleton, to conduct a surveillance on the home of Bob Sample—2342 Dayton Place. When Pendleton and his team arrived at Dayton Place they saw Sample standing in the front yard talking to a young blond woman. At the moment this team arrived, they saw the woman hand Bob a large burlap sack with the words "laundry" written in large white script on one side. Bob gave the woman a long hug and kiss on her cheek. The woman turned away and entered a taxi waiting at the curb. Officer Pendleton instructed three of the team members to follow the taxi.

As the officers followed the woman in the taxi one of them called the taxi dispatcher and were informed that the taxi was going to a 1665 Garland Avenue in Fayetteberg. The dispatcher also told the officers that this female passenger had made the same trip by taxi several times a day for the past two months. The three officers agreed that their suspicions were further aroused because drug dealers and "mules" commonly use taxis to avoid detection by the police.

As the young woman stepped out of the cab the team of uniformed officers walked up to her and asked for permission to speak with her. One of the officers also asked the taxi driver for permission to search the taxi for anything the woman might have left inside. The woman agreed to talk to the officers. She told them her name was Theresa Green. When asked where she was going, Green pointed to the address: 1665 Garland. Green was asked to produce some identification. She showed the officer her driver's license. The name on the Arkansas driver's license was Theresa Green, and it indicated her address was 1665 Garland Avenue and that she was born on February 1, 1984.

The officer asked Green whether anyone else lived at 1665 Garland. She said her kid sister, nineteen-year-old Dorothy Green, did. The officer then asked Green if she had any weapons on her. She told him that she had a knife in her purse, and he asked her to show him. Green opened her purse and pulled out knife with a three-inch blade. Upon seeing the knife the officer called for a policewoman to conduct a pat-down of Green. Ten minutes later a policewoman arrived and conducted a pat-down.

During this pat-down of Green the female officer felt a "big wad of cash." The female officer asked her how much money was in that roll of cash. Green told her "several hundred dollars." The male officer asked, "What else is in that purse?" Green told him that she had "a little weed" in it. The officer instructed her to dump the contents of her purse on the hood of the police car. The officer found two grams of marijuana in a small plastic bag. The officer arrested Ms. Green. Then, she was handcuffed and placed in the back seat of the police car.

The officers called Officer Pendleton to inform him of what had occurred to date and to advise him that the officers were going to knock on the door at 1665 Garland to corroborate Green's story. Green's sister, Dorothy, answered the door. After confirming her identification, the officers informed Dorothy that they had arrested her sister, Theresa, and told her that they had taken a large amount of money and some marijuana from Theresa. The officers asked for permission to search the house. Dorothy stepped to one side and ushered them in. When they entered the living room one of the officers saw a marijuana cigarette on the coffee table. That officer showed the others what he'd seen. The officer then asked Dorothy for permission to search the house. When she said that her sister (Theresa) had told her never to let strangers walk through her apartment, the officers said in unison, "We're the police!" "Besides," said one of the officers, "we can leave an officer in charge of maintaining the status quo until we get a warrant." Concerned that her four-year-old son, who would be returning from day care, would be upset by the police searching the house, she signed a consent form allowing the search. A search of the house revealed marijuana, cocaine, heroin, and drug paraphernalia. Theresa and Dorothy were charged with possession of illegal drugs with the intent to distribute.

Defendants are expected to file motions to suppress the evidence of possession of controlled substances. You are an associate prosecutor. Please provide your senior prosecutor with a memorandum of law (1) analyzing the key legal precedents that the defendants will likely use to support their motions, (2) isolating the most persuasive arguments distilled from those precedents, and (3) predicting how the court is likely to rule on these competing arguments.

LIST OF READINGS

1. The Fourth Amendment to the United States Constitution.
2. Federal Rules of Evidence Rule 401. Definition of Relevant Evidence.
3. Federal Rules of Evidence Rule 402. Relevant Evidence Generally Admissible; Irrelevant Evidence Inadmissible.
4. *United States v. Robinson*, 414 U.S. 218 (1973).
5. *Gustafson v. Florida*, 414 U.S. 260 (1973).
6. *Marron v. United States*, 275 U.S. 192 (1927).
7. *Go-Bart Importing Co. v. United States*, 282 U.S. 344 (1931).
8. *United States v. Lefkowitz*, 285 U.S. 452 (1932).
9. *Harris v. United States*, 331 U.S. 145 (1947).
10. *Trupiano v. United States*, 334 U.S. 699 (1948).
11. *Chimel v. United States*, 395 U.S. 752 (1969).

12. *New York v. Belton*, 453 U.S. 454 (1981).
13. *Thornton v. United States*, 541 U.S. 615 (2004).
14. *Arizona v. Gant*, 129 S. Ct. 1710 (2009).
15. *United States v. Rabinowitz*, 339 U.S. 56, 57 (1950).
16. *Knowles v. Iowa*, 525 U.S. 113 (1998).
17. *Katz v. United States*, 389 U.S. 347 (1967).
18. *Terry v. Ohio*, 392 U.S. 1 (1968).
19. *Alabama v. White*, 496 U.S. 325 (1990).
20. *Camara v. Municipal Court*, 387 U.S. 523 (1962).
21. *United States v. Cortez*, 449 U.S. 411 (1981).
22. *Sibron v. New York*, 392 U.S. 40 (1968).
23. *United States v. Arvizu*, 534 U.S. 266 (2002).
24. *Ornelas v. United States*, 517 U.S. 690 (1996).
25. *Illinois v. Wardlow*, 528 U.S. 119 (2000).
26. *Adams v. Williams*, 407 U.S. 143 (1972).
27. *Michigan v. Long*, 463 U.S. 1032 (1983).
28. *Pennsylvania v. Mimms*, 434 U.S. 106 (1977).
29. *Florida v. J.L.*, 529 U.S. 266 (2000).
30. *Hiibel v. Sixth Judicial Dist. Court*, 542 U.S. 177 (2004).
31. *California v. Hodari D*, 499 U.S. 621 (1991).
32. *Florida v. Bostick*, 501 U.S. 429 (1991).
33. *United States v. Drayton*, 536 U.S. 194 (2002).
34. *United States v. Mendenhall*, 446 U.S. 544 (1980).
35. *Brendlin v. California*, 551 U.S. 249 (2007).
36. *Wong Sun v. United States*, 371 U.S. 471 (1963).
37. *Maryland v. Buie*, 494 U.S. 325 (1990).
38. *Minnesota v. Dickerson,* 508 U.S. 366 (1993).
39. *Maryland v. King*, 133 S. Ct. 1958 (2013).
40. *Florence v. Board of Chosen Freeholders*, 132 S. Ct. 1510 (2012).

SAMPLE ESSAY

To: Senior Prosecutor
From: Associate Prosecutor
Re: Suppression Hearing in the Matter of Theresa and Dorothy Green—Possession of Controlled Substances (e.g., marijuana, cocaine, etc.)
Date:

In anticipation of motions to suppress evidence by the defendants named above, I have prepared this memorandum of law for your consideration. As you will discover this memorandum attempts to (1) identify the key legal precedents available to both sides, (2) isolate the most persuasive arguments distilled from those precedents, and (3) predict how the court is likely to rule on these competing arguments.

Obviously the defendant Theresa Green will claim that she was seized when three officers approached her and asked her pointed questions. That is, she will argue that in view of all the circumstances surrounding the incident, a reasonable person would have believed that he was not free to leave. And, because she will claim the officers did not have probable cause or reasonable suspicion, her seizure was unreasonable. Because of this alleged unreasonable seizure Green will contend that all the evidence taken from her purse, person, and house are fruits of that initial unlawful seizure. This tainted fruit, she will argue, should be suppressed pursuant to the exclusionary rule.

PART A. THE GENERAL RULE OF ADMISSIBILITY

Federal Rule of Evidence 401 provides that all relevant evidence is admissible except as otherwise provided by the Constitution of the United States. Because the Fourth Amendment to the United States Constitution prohibits unreasonable searches and seizures, any unreasonable search or seizure violates the Fourth Amendment. For example, the Supreme Court has held that a warrantless search of a citizen's property by an agent of the government violates the Fourth Amendment. More important, in order to make this Fourth Amendment protection effective the Supreme Court has held that evidence seized as a result of the unlawful search cannot constitute proof at trial against the victim of the search.

At the pretrial process, the judge must determine whether

(a) The defendant Green was "seized" under the Fourth Amendment; or
(b) She was engaged in a consensual encounter.

PART B. THE DISCUSSION

The focal point of the defendant's argument is her claim that the initial encounter between the three officers and her, as she stepped out of the taxi, was an unlawful seizure. Consequently, our most cogent response should inform the court that the United States Supreme Court has held that a police officer's act of approaching a citizen and asking a few questions in the process is a consensual encounter that does not implicate the Fourth Amendment. If the Fourth Amendment is not implicated, then the defendant is precluded from presenting argument about an unlawful seizure.

Simply stated the court will be asked to decide whether the initial encounter between Green and the three officers was consensual or a seizure. Even if the judge rejects our consensual encounter argument we may be able to present sufficient articulable facts to support a lawful *Terry* stop. Both issues will be examined in turn.

Consensual Encounter versus a Seizure

The seminal opinion defining when a police–citizen encounter becomes a seizure is *United States v. Mendenhall. Mendenhall* instructs that an encounter becomes a seizure only if, in view of all the circumstances surrounding the incident, a reasonable person would have believed that he was not free to leave. According to some members of the Court no seizure occurred in *Mendenhall* because:

> the events took place in the public concourse. The agents wore no uniforms and displayed no weapons. They did not summon the respondent to their presence, but instead approached her and identified themselves as federal agents. They requested

but did not demand to see respondent's identification and ticket. Such conduct, without more did not amount to an intrusion upon any constitutionally protected interests.

The facts in our hypothetical are virtually the same as in *Mendenhall* except that Green faced three uniformed officers on a public street instead of two plainclothes federal agents in an airport concourse. As in *Mendenhall*, we should be able to successfully argue that the three officers' conduct without more did not amount to a seizure.

Terry Stop and Interrogate

If we fail to persuade the court that the encounter between Green and the three officers was consensual, we should claim that Green was seized pursuant to *Hiibel v. Sixth Judicial District Court*. We should assert that the *Terry* stop was justified at its inception or that the officers had articulable facts or reasons for believing that criminal activity was afoot. In our hypothetical the officers had information from an anonymous informant that Bob Sample sold drugs and that he was usually accompanied during the sales by a young blond woman. When the officers arrived at Bob's house they saw a young blond woman, who fit the description provided in the anonymous letter, standing next to and talking to the suspect. Although the anonymous informant in this hypothetical did not predict future events as the anonymous informant reported in *Alabama v. White*, some of the informant's information was subsequently corroborated. Indeed, enough of the informant's information was corroborated allowing us reasonably claim that the officers' investigating stop was justified by some objective manifestation that the person stopped is, or is about to be, engaged in criminal activity.

Although the United States Supreme Court concedes that terms such as "articulable reasons" are not self-defining, it is clear, however, that when determining whether the police had enough articulable reasons or facts to make a lawful *Terry* stop, the Court has stated that a court must take into account the totality of the circumstances. Based upon the whole picture the detaining officers must have a particularized and objective basis for suspecting the particular person is engaged in a criminal activity. The facts in our case show the information in the anonymous letter has been, in part, corroborated. So, our officers had a particularized and objective basis for suspecting Theresa Green of criminal activity.

TOOLS FOR SELF-CRITICISM

The fractured *Mendenhall* Court graphically revealed that there was no definitive way to determine that an initial encounter resulted in a seizure under the Fourth Amendment. A person has been seized within the meaning of the Fourth Amendment only if, in view of all the circumstances surrounding the incident, a reasonable person would have believed that he was not free to leave. Based on this interpretation the Court looked to whether the citizen who was questioned remained free to disregard the questions and walk away. And the Court has explained that examples of seizures include the threatening presence of several officers, the display of a weapon by an officer, or some physical touching of a citizen's person. However, the Court has backed away from these examples.

Unfortunately, the prosecutor's memorandum neglected to consider that *Mendenhall*'s free-to-leave test has been reduced from a sufficient-to-show seizure test to only a necessary step in the process. In other words, where a police officer makes a show of authority that would convey to a reasonable person that he was not free to leave, the officer has failed to establish a seizure based on this showing alone. Today, *Hodari D* requires that this necessary step becomes sufficient to support a seizure only if the officer either restrains the liberty of the citizen or the citizen yields to that show of authority. In our hypothetical the police did not make a show of authority, nor did they restrain Green's liberty. Hence, there was no seizure under the old *Mendenhall* free-to-leave test, nor was there a seizure under *Hodari D*'s free-to-leave plus restraint of liberty or free to leave and a citizen's yield to a show of authority.

The prosecutor's memorandum also failed to discuss the separate seizure test fashioned by the Court in *Florida v. Bostick* and *United States v. Drayton*. Although the Court addressed several issues in both opinions, one query was answered in the same manner: whether *Mendenhall*'s free-to-leave test was the appropriate one for determining when a citizen has been seized on a bus. As the police in *Bostick* lacked reasonable suspicion to justify the seizure that occurred, the drugs found in Bostick's suitcase must have been suppressed as fruit of the poisonous tree. The *Bostick* Court concluded that *Mendenhall*'s free-to-leave test did not apply to a police–passenger encounter on a bus. That is, the Court opined that Bostick's movements on the bus were confined by his decision to take the bus, not by any actions of the police.

Even so, the *Bostick* Court refrained from deciding whether a seizure had occurred in that case. Instead the Court remanded the case to the Florida Supreme Court to decide the matter under the correct legal standard. In such a situation, the appropriate inquiry is whether a reasonable person would feel free to decline the officer's request or otherwise terminate the encounter. The facts of our hypothetical do not, except for the three officers to one citizen ratio, invite a discussion of the *Bostick/Drayton* variety. So, there is no seizure under any applicable test. More important, where there is no seizure the Fourth Amendment is not implicated.

SPECIAL NEEDS AND REASONABLENESS UNDER THE FOURTH AMENDMENT

8

OPENING REMARKS

The Court has held that the language in the Fourth Amendment guarantees, among other things, the privacy of persons against arbitrary and unreasonable search and seizures by the federal government. Moreover, the Court has determined that the Fourteenth Amendment extends these Fourth Amendment protections to citizens against the acts of *state* officers, including public school officials.

The text of the Fourth Amendment, according to the Court, indicates that the ultimate measure of the constitutionality of a governmental search is reasonableness. The Court has also opined that where a search is undertaken by law enforcement officials to discover evidence of criminal wrongdoing, reasonableness generally requires the obtaining of a judicial warrant. Pursuant to the text of the Fourth Amendment, a warrant must be supported by probable cause. Even so, the Court has crafted another well-defined exception to the Fourth Amendment's warrant and probable cause requirements. This exception is based on the "special needs of the government beyond the normal need for law enforcement." For example, the Court has held that (1) government employers and supervisors may conduct warrantless work-related searches of an employee's desk and office without a showing of probable cause; (2) state public school officials may conduct warrantless searches of a public school student's person or property on something less than probable cause; (3) the Federal Railroad Administration may promulgate regulations that, among other things, compel employees, who were involved in major train accidents or incidents, to submit to urine collection and testing; and (4) the United States Custom Service may require urinalysis test from employees who seek promotion to sensitive positions within the service, in order to prevent the promotion of drug users to those positions. Although each of these examples of special needs deserves additional examination and discussion, our discussion begins with the seminal opinion, *New Jersey v. T.L.O.*

A high school teacher alleged that she discovered T.L.O. and another fourteen-year-old high school girl smoking cigarettes in the school lavatory; T.L.O. denied the charge. Indeed, T.L.O. later denied the same charge to a vice principal of the high school. Suspecting that T.L.O. was lying, the vice principal conducted a warrantless search of T.L.O.'s purse. During this warrantless search, the principal discovered money, drug paraphernalia, marijuana, and two letters implicating T.L.O. in drug trafficking. T.L.O.'s motion, to exclude this discovered evidence as fruits of a Fourth Amendment violation, failed.

In *T.L.O.*, the Court concluded that it was satisfied that the search of T.L.O.'s purse did not violate the Fourth Amendment. In order to reach this conclusion the Court had to consider or resolve several issues, and it had to embrace or establish several legal principles. First, the Court held that the Fourth Amendment's prohibition of unreasonable searches and seizures applied to searches conducted by public school officials, primarily because (1) the Fourth Amendment applies to the states through the Fourteenth Amendment, and the actions of public school officials are subject to the limits placed on state action by the Fourteenth Amendment; and (2) the Court has never limited the Fourth Amendment's prohibition on unreasonable searches and seizures to operations conducted by the police. Rather, the Court has long spoken of the Fourth Amendment's strictures as restraints imposed upon governmental action. In carrying out searches and other disciplinary functions pursuant to such policies, school officials act as representatives of the state, not merely as surrogates for the parents, and they cannot claim the parents' immunity from the strictures of the Fourth Amendment.

Second, even though the Fourth Amendment applies to searches conducted by public school officials, that is merely a necessary step in the analysis, but not a sufficient one. In order to determine whether a search conducted by a public school official was reasonable requires balancing the need to search against the invasion that the search entails. On one side of the balance are arrayed the individual's legitimate expectations of privacy and personal security; on the other, the government's need for effective methods to deal with breaches of public order.

Third, in a school setting a court must strike the balance between the school child's legitimate expectations of privacy and the school's equally legitimate need to maintain an environment in which learning can take place. Again, in a school setting there must be some easing of the restrictions to which searches by public authorities are ordinarily subject. For example, the warrant requirement is deemed unsuited for the school environment, because, the Court concludes, requiring a teacher to obtain a warrant before searching a child suspected of an infraction would unduly interfere with the maintenance of the swift and informal disciplinary procedures needed in the schools. On this basis alone, special needs exist in the public school setting.

Fourth, as with the warrant requirement the Court opines that the school environment is unsuited for the probable cause requirement, because, the Court contends, probable cause is not an irreducible requirement of a valid search. According to the Court, the Fourth Amendment requires reasonable searches and seizures. As the warrant and probable cause requirements merely bear on the reasonableness of a search, there are other ways to achieve reasonableness. Indeed, many searches have been considered reasonable even though they did not rise to the level of probable cause.

As a consequence, the Court concluded that the legality of a search of a student should depend simply on the reasonableness, under all the circumstances, of the search. To determine the reasonableness of such a search the Court adopted a two-step inquiry: first, one must consider whether the action was justified at its inception; and second, one must determine whether the search as actually conducted was reasonably related in scope to the circumstances that justified the interference in the first place.

The *T.L.O.* Court offered the bench and bar a few practical guidelines for its two-part test: under ordinary circumstances, a search of a student by a teacher or other school official will be justified at its inception when there are reasonable grounds for suspecting that the search will turn up evidence that the student has violated or is violating either the law or the rules of the school. Such a search will be permissible in its scope when the measures adopted are reasonably related to the objectives of the search and not excessively intrusive in light of the age and sex of the student and the nature of the infraction. These practical guidelines do not consider the appropriate standard to apply when trying to determine the reasonableness of searches conducted by a public school official searching in concert with a police officer. So, a search conducted by the police with a school official's assistance was not determined by *T.L.O.* and has not been otherwise considered by the Court. More important, the Court conceded that it did not decide whether individualized suspicion is an essential element of the reasonableness standard. And, the Court's decision did not create a hierarchy of rules where some rules were more trivial than others. As a consequence, any rule violation may lead to a warrantless search of a public school child.

The *T.L.O.* Court acknowledged that the reasonable grounds standard applied by the New Jersey Supreme Court in its consideration of this question was not substantially different from its own standard. Still, the Court rejected what it termed the state court's somewhat crabbed notion of reasonableness. Curiously, however, the Court's conclusion that the initial and further searches of T.L.O.'s purse were reasonable did not appear to rely on the state's reasonableness standard, or on its own standard. In fact, the Court based its conclusion, in part, on Federal Rule of Evidence 401. "Evidence having any tendency to make the existence of any fact is of consequence… more probable or less probable than it would be without the evidence."

The *T.L.O.* Court appears to read Federal Rule of Evidence 401 as dispositive. That is, because T.L.O. had denied the accusation that she had violated a school rule by smoking in the lavatory, the Court reasoned that relevant evidence is a type that (1) need not conclusively prove that point, but that it need (2) only have a tendency to prove that point. Thus, the Court opined that the relevance of T.L.O.'s possession of cigarettes to the question of whether she had been smoking and to the credibility of her denial that she smoked supplied the necessary "nexus" between the item searched for and the infraction under investigation. Moreover, the Court concluded that the vice principal had acted reasonably when he initially examined T.L.O.'s purse in order to confirm that it contained cigarettes. The vice principal, the Court further explained, acted reasonably because a teacher told him that T.L.O. and her companion had violated a school rule by smoking in the lavatory. The Court determined that the vice principal's suspicion that T.L.O.'s purse might contain cigarettes was reasonable. As the Court saw it, the vice principal's suspicion about the contents of T.L.O.'s purse was the sort of common-sense conclusion about human behavior upon which practical people, including government officials, are entitled to rely. Based on the preceding analysis, the Court concluded that the search of T.L.O.'s purse was reasonable.

Special Needs and a Strip Search of a Public School Student

Similar to the search of T.L.O.'s purse, the Court has held in *Safford Unified School District #1 v. Redding* that under certain circumstances it is reasonable for a public school official to conduct a warrantless search of a school student's backpack and outer clothing. The Court found that if a student is reasonably suspected of giving out contraband pills, she is reasonably suspected of carrying them on her person and in the carryall (backpack) that has become an item of student uniform in most places. However, under these same facts the Court held that it was constitutionally unreasonable for a public official to command the school student to remove her clothes down to her underwear, and then demand that she pull out her bra and the elastic band on her underwear. In addition, the Court considered it inconsequential for Fourth Amendment purposes that the school officials claimed that they did not see any part of the student's body when she pulled her undergarments away from her body.

Although the *Safford* Court noted that the indignity of the search alone would not make it unreasonable, the indignity would implicate the rule of reasonableness as stated in *T.L.O.* that the search as actually conducted be reasonably related in scope to the circumstances that justified the interference in the first place. Thus, reasoned the Court, the scope of the search will be considered reasonable when it is not excessively intrusive in light of the age and sex of the student and the nature of the infraction. Here the Court concluded that the content of the suspicion failed to match the degree of intrusion. The Court observed that the school official knew beforehand that the pills were over-the- counter pain relievers and were therefore only a limited threat.

Suspicionless-Searches Based on Special Needs

Since its suspicion-based *T.L.O.* opinion the Court has also upheld suspicionless searches where the government had a substantial and a legitimate interest in (1) regulating railroad safety; (2) controlling which employees could be promoted to safety-sensitive or high-risk positions; or (3) preventing drug addiction among public school athletes, or students who participate in other extracurricular activities. All of these suspicionless searches involved the government collecting and subsequently analyzing urine taken from citizens. This act of collecting and analyzing urine implicated the Fourth Amendment.

In these suspicionless-search cases the Court has emphasized that concluding that the Fourth Amendment applies merely begins the appropriate inquiry. In order to determine the reasonableness of such a suspicionless search a court must conduct a two-step analysis. First, what is reasonable depends on all the circumstances surrounding the search or seizure and the nature of the search or seizure itself. For example, although a urine test is not invasive of the body, it does require employees (or students) to perform an excretory function traditionally shielded by great privacy. As a result, the Court has noted that a urine test raises additional privacy concerns. One such concern is whether school officials (or employers) should monitor the student during the collection process in order to insure the integrity of the test. How closely and carefully to monitor the student are issues of reasonableness. The Court has determined that such a collection process is minimally intrusive and therefore reasonable if there is no monitor present.

The Court has, however, emphasized that the proffered special need for drug testing must be substantially important enough to override the individual's acknowledged privacy interest, and sufficiently vital to suppress the Fourth Amendment's normal requirement of individualized suspicion. For example, in *Chandler v. Miller*, the Court held that the State of Georgia's requirement that candidates for public office must submit to drug testing was unconstitutional because

> Georgia asserts no evidence of a drug problem among the State's elected officials, those officials typically do not perform high risk, safety-sensitive tasks, and the required certification immediately aids no interdiction effort. The need revealed, in short, is symbolic, not special as the term draws meaning from our case law.

Similarly, the Court in *Ferguson v. City of Charleston* held that a state hospital's warrantless drug tests on urine samples collected from maternity patients suspected of using cocaine were unconstitutional suspicionless searches

> because the hospital [sought] to justify its authority to conduct drug tests and to turn the results over to law enforcement agents without the knowledge or consent of the patients.

The Court concluded that

"The critical difference between those four drug-testing cases and this one, however, lies in the nature of the special needs asserted as a justification for the warrantless searches. In each of those earlier cases, the special need that was advanced as a justification for the absence of a warrant or individualized suspicion was one divorced from the State's general interest in law enforcement."

Suspicionless Automobile Roadblocks and Special Needs

In *Delaware v. Prouse*, the United States Supreme Court held that, among other things, it was unreasonable under the Fourth Amendment to (1) make a warrantless suspicionless stop of an automobile, and (2) detain its driver in order to check his driver's license and the registration of his automobile. Despite this holding, the Court informed Delaware that its holding did not preclude all suspicionless/warrantless stops of this kind. The Court also recognized that other roadblocks were not precluded by this opinion. The Court stated that its opinion did not cast doubt on the permissibility of roadside truck weigh stations and inspection checkpoints, at which some vehicles may be subject to further detention for safety and regulatory inspection than are others.

In *Michigan Department of State Police v. Sitz*, the Court had to determine whether the Michigan Department of State Police's highway sobriety checkpoints were unconstitutional or whether the checkpoint served special government needs. The Court upheld the reasonableness of Michigan's suspicionless sobriety checkpoint by relying on, in part, (1) a balancing test derived from prior precedents, and (2) a three-part test found in *Brown v. Texas*. Employing *Brown*'s three factors the Court found that the sobriety checkpoint was constitutional because (1) the special governmental need (beyond the normal need for law enforcement) was significant (preventing drunk driving); (2) the checkpoint was conducted pursuant to guidelines that minimized police discretion, and (3) the sobriety checkpoint effectively advanced the governmental interest because it resulted in the arrest of 1.5 percent of the persons driving through the checkpoint.

However, in 2000 the Supreme Court placed some limits on suspicionless government checkpoints. The Court noted in *City of Indianapolis v. Edmond* that it had never approved of a suspicionless checkpoint program whose primary purpose was to detect evidence of ordinary criminal wrongdoing. As a result, the Court held that because the primary purpose of the Indianapolis narcotics checkpoint program was to uncover evidence of ordinary criminal wrongdoing, the program contravened the Fourth Amendment. Such stops require individualized suspicion.

However, the Court did identify two exceptions to its ban on suspicionless checkpoints to uncover evidence of ordinary criminal wrongdoing: (1) an appropriately tailored roadblock set up to thwart an imminent terrorist attack, or (2) a roadblock set up to catch a dangerous criminal who is likely to flee by way of a particular route.

In *Illinois v. Lidster*, the Supreme Court had to decide whether a suspicionless checkpoint was constitutional when the police established it to obtain information about a recent hit-and-run fatality. The Court determined that this suspicionless information- seeking highway stop was reasonable or constitutional because it satisfied the *Brown v. Texas* three-prong balancing test: (1) the gravity of the public concerns served by the suspicionless stop, (2) the degree to which the stop advances that public interest, and (3) the severity (or lack of severity) of the stop's interference with the individual's liberty.

Community Caretaking, Inventory Searches, and Special Needs

The Court has held that a warrantless (and suspicionless) search of an impounded car in actual police custody is not unreasonable when the search was conducted pursuant to police regulations designed to insure the safety of the car and the owner's property. Similarly, where state health regulations required the police to retain a car in their custody until a forfeiture proceeding, the Court opined that it would be unreasonable to hold that the police, who had to retain the car in their custody, for such a length of time, had no right, even for their own protection, to search it without a warrant.

Based on these early decisions, the Court held that even if the police did not have actual physical custody, but the car was stored at a site pursuant to police instructions, it was constitutionally reasonable to search the car without a warrant. The Court upheld the warrantless search of the impounded car, in part, because of the police concern for the safety of the general public who might be endangered if an intruder removed a revolver (that was suspected to be in the trunk) from the trunk of the vehicle. Moreover, the Court did not find the warrantless search unreasonable even if the search could have been accomplished by less intrusive means. The Court cautioned that the need to conduct these warrantless impoundments and searches of vehicles for want of a better term may be described as *community caretaking* functions, totally divorced from the detection, investigation, or acquisition of evidence relating to the violation of a criminal statute.

The Court has concluded that in the interest of public safety and as a part of what it has called community caretaking functions, vehicles are taken into police custody for a myriad of reasons. Generally these caretaking procedures follow a routine practice of securing and inventorying the contents of an automobile. As a result, the Court has emphasized that these caretaking procedures have developed in response to three distinct needs: the protection of the owner's property while it remains in police custody, the protection of the police against claims or disputes over lost or stolen property, and the protection of the police against potential danger.

When the police were indisputably engaged in a caretaking search of a lawfully impounded car because it was illegally parked for an extended period, and the owner was not present to make other arrangements for the safekeeping of his belongings, the warrantless search of that car was considered reasonable. However, if the alleged inventory search was a pretext for concealing an investigatory police motive such a search is unreasonable under the Fourth Amendment. The reasonableness of a suspicionless search may be denied if the motive for the search was pretextual.

Inventory Searches

The Court has rejected the notion that government activity that was less intrusive to an individual's privacy interest was the only way to measure the reasonableness of that activity. Although there were less intrusive means available for preserving an arrestee's property or for protecting the police against claims of lost or stolen property, the Court held that it was not unreasonable for the police, as part of the standardized procedure incident to incarcerating an arrested person, to search any container or article in his possession, in accordance with established inventory procedures. Indeed, the Court has decided that such an inventory search is an exception to the warrant requirement. Consequently, in order to determine the reasonableness of an inventory search the Court held that courts must balance the intrusion on an individual's Fourth Amendment interests against its promotion of legitimate governmental interests. In significant part, the governmental interests supporting inventory searches are justified by the same distinct needs identified in the community caretaking—car impoundment cases—the protection of the (1) owner's property while it remains in police custody, and (2) police against false claims of lost property or against dangerous instrumentalities. On the other hand, the Court has held that the police are not required as a condition of the search to balance an individual's privacy interests in a container against the government's interest that the container was a repository for dangerous items, before conducting a warrantless inventory search of that container.

Despite its emphasis on the police conducting warrantless inventory searches pursuant to standardized criteria, the Court in *Florida v. Wells* has also left room for the police to use discretion when conducting such warrantless searches. The language by the Court provides specifically that the police may exercise discretion only pursuant to standardized criteria, and that this principle demands that such an inventory search must not be a ruse for a general rummaging in order to discover incriminating evidence. Regrettably, the Court's dicta has in *Wells* virtually eviscerated the clarity of the limits on the police use of discretion when conducting warrantless inventory searches pursuant to standardized criteria.

HYPOTHETICAL

Police Chief Marck Jackson (hereafter "Chief Jackson") of the Fayetteberg Police Department found the following anonymous letter under his office door around 7:30 am on May 29, 2010:

> I am an employee at Wal-Market Super Center on 12th Street in Fayetteberg. You should know that several people on the Wal-Market management staff at this store are selling powdered cocaine to kids at Fayetteberg High School and Romney Jr. High. They also have two white male high school students working for them at Fayetteberg High. One of the students is a tall lanky guy named "DV" and a short round guy named "Fireplug." Both students are high school juniors. Two kids at Romney Jr. High died from overdosing on this toxic dope. The street name of this cocaine is "Triple H."
>
> By the way, some of these Wal-Market managers are quite well-known in the community. Two of them are named "Bob." You know them well! They brag on how they've made so much money selling drugs and how they can hide it through their

> regular jobs. They sell the cocaine from the employee restrooms at the 12th Street store. They also use the employee lockers to store (and sometimes sell from) the drugs. The drugs are sometimes stored in their cars.

Chief Jackson conducted a search of police files to determine if any students from Romney Jr. High had recently died of toxic drugs. After a two-hour search he found records of three recent deaths by toxic drugs. Two of these deaths were of seventh graders at Canal Jr. High in Roland, Arkansas. The other death was of an eighth grader at Romney Jr. High. He also had several tips from reliable informants that "DV" and "Fireplug" sold drugs in the neighborhood.

After this search and gathering the information from the tipster about "DV" and "Fireplug," he called the Chief Security Officer at the Fayetteberg High School, John Walker. Officer Walker was also a sergeant in the Fayetteberg Police Department. Officer Walker split his time between regular police patrols in his city and security at the high school. This was Officer Walker's tenth year as a security officer at the high school. As Chief Jackson had originally assigned Officer Walker to the high school security detail, he felt that he could collect some helpful information from him.

Officer Walker told the Chief that he did not know "DV" or "Fireplug" but that he'd keep a "lookout" and a "listen-out" for them. The Chief asked Officer Walker to question both boys about drug dealing in the Fayetteberg city limits—if he could identify them. Officer Walker agreed to do so. The following morning before the start of the first class Officer Walker saw the usual gathering of ten to twelve students across the street from the school in an area dubbed by the students "Yo Tabacco Fix-on." This was a notorious spot for student smokers. Of course, some students who did not smoke hung out there as well.

On this date Officer Walker saw four women and eight men at the "Yo Tabacco Fix-on." He could see all four women smoking cigarettes and one guy smoking a cigar. He recognized only two of the women: a sophomore, Monica Pugh, and a freshman, Jessica Turner. When the chimes sounded for the beginning of the first class, the group of students from the "Yo Tabacco Fix-on" spot crossed the street and entered the Fayetteberg High School grounds. For the past year it had been the routine practice of the Fayetteberg High School Police security force to detain all the students, including Monica Pugh and Jessica Turner; pat down their outer clothing; and search their backpacks for tobacco and tobacco products. This routine practice usually occurred twice per week. As Walker had to search four high school girls he summoned Officer Francine Adams and Officer Barb Crain to assist him. The search of the four women did not disclose any tobacco or tobacco products.

Officer Walker noticed that one of the eight boys was very short and built like a, well, "fireplug." Taking a chance, Officer Walker yelled, "Say, Fireplug! Come on over here, Hoss!" The fat round boy walked immediately to Walker and said, "Yes, sir." Officer Walker looked down at the young boy and said, "What is the name your parents gave you, Hoss?" "William Tatum," he replied. Officer Walker said, "I think 'Bill' or 'William' sounds better than 'Fireplug'! What do you think?" Fireplug just shrugged his shoulders.

During his search of "Fireplug" Officer Walker found thirty packs of extra-light Zig-Zag paper, four ounces of marijuana, $500 cash in ten and twenty dollar bills, and a list of student names with dollar amounts and dates next to them. William Tatum was promptly arrested.

The school policy at Fayetteberg High School prohibits smoking, tobacco products, contraband, and cigarettes on school property. As a result, Officer Walker is authorized to conduct searches for items that violate that policy. Officer Walker has been authorized by the chief school official—Principal Maureen Johnson. Principal Johnson has authorized the police security officers to conduct warrantless searches on randomly selected days of all students entering the school grounds from the "Yo Tabacco Fix-on" spot across the street from the school.

As a consequence of the items found in the search, the state petitioned to have William Tatum tried as an adult for possession of marijuana with the intent to distribute.

Defendant has filed a Motion to Exclude the marijuana, cash, list of student names, and various packs of paper, pursuant to an alleged unlawful search and seizure. You are an associate prosecutor. Please provide your senior prosecutor with a memorandum of law: (1) analyzing the key legal precedents that the defendant will likely use to support his motions, (2) isolating the most persuasive arguments distilled from those precedents, and (3) predicting how the court is likely to rule on these competing arguments.

LIST OF READINGS

1. The Fourth Amendment to the United States Constitution.
2. The Fourteenth Amendment to the United States Constitution.
3. Federal Rules of Evidence Rule 401. Definition of Relevant Evidence.
4. Federal Rules of Evidence Rule 402. Relevant Evidence Generally Admissible; Irrelevant Evidence Inadmissible.
5. *Skinner v. Railway Labor Executive Ass'n*, 489 U.S. 602 (1989).
6. *Vernonia School District 47j v. Acton*, 515 U.S. 646 (1995).
7. *Elkins v. United States*, 364 U.S. 206 (1960).
8. *New Jersey v. T.L.O.*, 469 U.S. 325, 340–42 (1985).
9. *Safford Univied School District #1 v. Redding*, 557 U.S. 364 (2009).
10. *City of Ontario v. Quon*, 130 S. Ct. 2619 (2010).
11. *National Treasury Employees Union v. Von Raab*, 489 U.S. 656, 672 (1989).
12. *Ferguson v. City of Charleston*, 532 U.S. 67 (2001).
13. *Board of Education of Independent School District No. 92 v. Earls*, 536 U.S. 822, 838 (2002).
14. Robert D. Dodson, Ten Years of Randomized Jurisprudence: Amending the Special Needs Doctrine, 51 S.C. L. Rev. 258 (2000).
15. Nancy J. Flatt-Moore, Public Schools and Urinalysis: Assessing the Validity of Indiana Public Schools Student Drug Testing Policies after *Vernonia*, 1998 B.Y.U. Educ. & L.J. 239, 252 (1998).
16. *State v. Prouse*, 382 A.2d 1359, 1364 (1978)).
17. *Michigan Department of State Police v. Sitz*, 496 U.S. 444 (1990).
18. *Brown v. Texas*, 443 U.S. 47, 51 (1979).
19. *Harris v. United States*, 390 U.S. 234 (1968).
20. *Cooper v. California*, 386 U.S. 58 (1967).
21. *Cady v. Dombrowski*, 413 U.S. 433 (1973).

22. *South Dakota v. Opperman*, 428 U.S. 364 (1976).
23. *Illinois v. Lafayette*, 462 U.S. 640, 647 (1983).
24. *Dady v. Dombrowski*, 413 U.S. 433 (1973).
25. *Colorado v. Bertine*, 479 U.S. 367, 374–75 (1987).
26. *Florida v. Wells*, 495 U.S. 1, 4 (1990).
27. *United States v. Martinez-Fuerte*, 428 U.S. 543, 560–61 (1976).

SAMPLE ESSAY

To: Senior Prosecutor
From: Associate Prosecutor
Re: Suppression Hearing—[*State v. William ("Bill") Tatum*]
Defendant's motions to exclude marijuana, cash, list of student names and various packs of paper pursuant to an alleged unlawful search and seizure
Date:

In anticipation of the above-described motions-in-limine by the defendant, I have prepared the following memorandum of law for your consideration. As you will discover this memorandum attempts to (1) identify the key legal precedents that the defendant will use to support his likely motions under the facts set out below, (2) isolate the most persuasive arguments distilled from these precedents that he is likely to assert (and our counterarguments to them), and (3) predict how the court is likely to rule on these competing arguments.

Although the defendant will primarily argue that Security Officer Walker lacked individualized or particularized suspicion to make a lawful arrest ("seizure"), he may also claim that the leading United States Supreme Court opinion upholding the warrantless search of a school child does not support the warrantless seizure of that child by a non-school official. In any event, whether the trial court considers the defendant's argument, claim, or both the defendant's objective is to persuade the court to exclude the incriminating evidence seized as a fruit of an unlawful search and seizure. By employing the language and rationale of the majority in the seminal *New Jersey v. T.L.O.* opinion we should successfully counter the defendant's individualized suspicion argument.

First, the *T.L.O.* Court held that in order (1) to help school officials maintain order and security, and (2) for courts to strike the balance between a school child's legitimate expectations of privacy and a school's equally legitimate need to maintain an environment for learning, the school setting requires some easing of the restrictions to which searches by public authorities are ordinarily subject. The Court eased the restriction on searches by public school officials by eliminating the warrant and probable cause requirements as the test for determining the reasonableness of a search.

Here, contrary to the defendant's argument *T.L.O.* allows us to show the trial court that the legality of a search of a student depends simply on its reasonableness, under all the circumstances. Pursuant to this general principle, *T.L.O.* empowers a trial court to determine reasonableness under all the circumstances by applying a two-pronged test. A court is permitted to determine reasonableness under this two-pronged test by evaluating whether the search was (1) reasonable at its inception, and (2) reasonably related in scope to the circumstances that justified the interference in the first place. As a result, our judge must determine the reasonableness under *T.L.O.*'s first prong: that is, was the search of William Tatum a/k/a "Fireplug" justified at its inception.

To determine whether a search was justified at its inception *T.L.O.* provides that under ordinary circumstances the search of a student by a teacher or other school official will be justified at its inception when there are reasonable grounds for suspecting that the search will turn up evidence that the student has violated or is violating either the law or the rules of the school. Because Officer Walker lacked reasonable grounds for suspecting or individualized suspicion that evidence would turn up on the defendant, the defendant will argue that the search was unreasonable. Although this argument has some superficial appeal, it ultimately fails under *T.L.O.* The *T.L.O.* Court emphasized that the court did not decide whether individualized suspicion is an essential element of the reasonableness standard adopted for searches by school authorities. In other contexts, however, the Court has held that although some quantum of individualized suspicion is usually a prerequisite to a constitutional search or seizure, the Fourth Amendment imposes no irreducible requirement of such suspicion.

Despite a lack of individualized suspicion our judge may determine that Officer Walker conducted a reasonable search and seizure at the inception of the encounter with the defendant. For example, the Court has held that where a quantity of drugs and cash were found in a lawfully stopped car, the policeman may reasonable infer that the two passengers were engaged in the common enterprise of drug dealing and concealing the fruits of that crime. Likewise, a high school student, who congregates with other high school students in a place notoriously and exclusively used by students to smoke cigarettes, will often be engaged in the common enterprise of smoking cigarettes.

Still, we should expect the defendant to argue that to uphold this search as reasonable would be tantamount to finding the defendant guilty of smoking merely because he was associating with smokers. It is true that the Court has held that a warrant to search a public tavern did not, without individualized suspicion, give the police the authority to pat down any patron for weapons. However, unlike the case involving the search of a patron in a public tavern, the circumstances of this case give the police some suspicion toward anyone of the persons who congregated at the Yo Tobacco Fix-on.

Second, the defendant may claim that *T.L.O.*'s *two-step* test does not apply when, as here, the police officers (and not the school officials) initiated and conducted the search and seizure. Accordingly the defendant will argue that the officer was required to show individualized suspicion. Contrary to the defendant's argument *T.L.O.* specifically declined to consider the nature of the Fourth Amendment review when a search is conducted by school officials in conjunction with or at the behest of law enforcement agencies, more permitted by, the court stated that it expressed no opinion on that question. Although some courts have applied *T.L.O.*'s reasonableness test to searches conducted by school officials in conjunction with police agents, searches conducted solely by police agents on public school grounds will be governed by the warrant and probable cause requirements. Even so, we should still prevail because probable cause or suspicion may be reasonably inferred from the defendant being engaged in the common enterprise of smoking cigarettes.

Once the trial court balances the defendant-child's legitimate expectation of privacy against the school's equally legitimate need to maintain an environment for learning, the court should uphold the search and seizure as reasonable under all the circumstances.

TOOLS FOR SELF-CRITICISM

Although *New Jersey v. T.L.O.* is presented as the dispositive opinion, the key issue controlling this hypothetical was not addressed in *T.L.O.* The Court in *T.L.O.* specifically declined to consider the nature of a Fourth Amendment review when a search is conducted by school officials in conjunction with or at the behest of law enforcement agencies. The court expressed no opinion on that question. So, the state has at least an even chance to prevail on this argument. Of course the level of suspicion required is determined by whether it is a police-initiated action requiring probable cause or a *special needs* action initiated by school officials requiring something less than probable cause.

In any event, as our facts conclusively show that the school officials neither conducted the searches on their own initiative nor pursuant to the request of the police, the lesser standard may apply. As a result, the prosecutor may prevail.

THE FIFTH AMENDMENT PRIVILEGE

9

OPENING REMARKS

The language comprising the privilege against self-incrimination is a meager component of the Fifth Amendment text: "nor shall [a person] be compelled in any criminal case to be a witness against himself."

Although the language of the privilege is limited, the court has interpreted this language according to several points of analysis: (1) general considerations, (2) *"shall be compelled,"* (3) *"in any criminal case,"*(4) to be a witness, and (5) against himself. Some general considerations and each of these points shall be examined seriatim.

As early as 1807, in *Brown v. Walker*, after considering the validity of asserting that right before a grand jury, Chief Justice John Marshall identified a few broad principles found in the privilege against self-incrimination.

(a) When the government asks a citizen a question, it is the Court's role to consider and to decide whether an answer implicates the privilege;
(b) If the judge decides that an answer will not implicate the privilege, then an answer from the citizen will not violate the privilege;
(c) Still, despite the foregoing principles (a) and (b), the testifying citizen must ultimately decide whether a direct answer to it may incriminate himself;
(d) The presiding judge cannot help the testifying citizen decide whether to testify because the citizen would lose the privilege by disclosing it to the judge;
(e) Once the testifying citizen states under oath that an answer will incriminate him, the judge may not demand more of him; and
(f) An answer provided by a testifying citizen may implicate the privilege even if standing alone it would not appear to incriminate him. That is, the privilege is implicated as long as the answer is a link in the chain of testimony that might form a necessary and essential part of a crime.

Nor Shall Be Compelled

The Court has held that it is a violation of the Fifth Amendment privilege against compelling testimony from a citizen for (1) a state attorney to use at the subsequent criminal prosecution incriminating answers made by police officers pursuant to a state statute that threatened to remove them from office if they refused to testify, (2) a city to discharge city employees pursuant to a city charter that authorized dismissal of city employees for refusing to waive their constitutional privilege against self-incrimination, (3) a state attorney to notify various contracting authorities that licensed architects were disqualified from contracting with the state because these architects refused to waive their Fifth Amendment right against self-incrimination, and (4) a state to prosecute and convict a citizen with his own testimony that was elicited under a threat of contempt by a United States Senate Committee investigating criminal activity. Even so, the Court has held that some forms of compelled testimony do not violate the Fifth Amendment privilege.

Immunity Statutes

The United States Supreme Court has noted that immunity statutes were written to provide a rational accommodation between the imperatives of the Fifth Amendment privilege and the legitimate demands of government to compel citizens to testify. Providing immunity against prosecution was important because sometimes the only persons capable of giving useful testimony were those implicated in the crime. Based on this analysis, the Court was required to decide which immunity was as comprehensive as the Fifth Amendment privilege.

First, in *Counselmen v. Hitchcock*, the Court held that an immunity statute is not a full substitute for the Fifth Amendment privilege if it cannot protect a testifying citizen against the use of the immunized testimony (1) to convict the citizen, and (2) as a source of information that leads to other incriminating evidence. Accordingly, use immunity alone was not considered coextensive with the Fifth Amendment privilege.

Second, the Court has held that the use-derivative use immunity is coextensive with the Fifth Amendment privilege and therefore is sufficient to compel testimony over a claim of the privilege; the Court noted that immunity from use and derivative use leaves the witness and the federal government in substantially the same position as if the witness had claimed the privilege. Pursuant to use-derivative use immunity a prosecutor is prohibited from using the immunized testimony either directly or indirectly against the testifying citizen. However, a prosecutor may prosecute the testifying witness with any evidence that is not connected to the immunized testimony, by establishing that he had an independent source for the disputed (unconnected) evidence.

Third, transactional immunity has been deemed more than coextensive with the Fifth Amendment privilege, because it affords absolute immunity against future prosecution for the offense that was the subject of the interrogation. Indeed, the Court considers transactional immunity to be broader than the Fifth Amendment privilege, because such an immunized citizen cannot subsequently be prosecuted with evidence from an independent source. As a result, the defendant will prefer transactional immunity, but the prosecutor will usually limit the offer to use-derivative use immunity. If the defendant declines to accept an offer of immunity, he may be subject to incarceration pending his compliance or the expiration of the grand jury's term.

Any Criminal Case

The Fifth Amendment provides that no one shall be compelled in any criminal *case* to be a witness against himself. Although the phrase "in any criminal case" may reasonably appear to refer to the time and nature of the particular proceedings where the questions are posed, the Court has rejected this notion. The phrase "a criminal case," the Court has determined, must have a broad construction in favor of the right it was intended to secure. Whenever the testifying citizen's answers create a real and appreciable danger that the statements could be used in a criminal prosecution or could lead to other evidence that might be used against the testifying citizen, the privilege applies.

However, in *United States v. Balsys*, the Court held that the Fifth Amendment does not apply to a resident alien's fear that his compelled testimony would be used to prosecute him in a foreign country, primarily because the Court read the compelled self-incrimination clause contextually as apparently providing a witness with the right against compelled self-incrimination when reasonably fearing prosecution by the government (the United States) whose power the clause limits, but not otherwise.

Early in its history, the Court has maintained that there are apparent exceptions to the Fifth Amendment privilege based upon the idea that if the testimony sought cannot possibly be used as a basis for or in aid of a criminal prosecution against the witness, the rule ceases to apply. For example, a testifying citizen may not assert the privilege where (1) he has elected to waive it, (2) the question posed relates to a crime barred by the statute of limitations, (3) an answer to the question posed may only disgrace him, or (4) the testifying citizen has received a pardon for the charged offense.

When determining whether the Fifth Amendment privilege applies, the Court has concluded that the distinction between a civil penalty and a criminal penalty is of some constitutional import. Moreover, the Court has emphasized that whether a particular statutorily defined penalty is civil or criminal is a matter of statutory construction. In order to engage in this statutory construction, the Court requires a two-step analysis. First, a court must determine whether Congress intended to specifically designate a penalty as civil or criminal. Second, even where Congress has specifically intended to establish a civil penalty, a further inquiry must be conducted. That is, a court must discover whether the statutory scheme was so punitive either in purpose or effect as to negate that intention.

To Be a Witness against Himself

In *Schmerber v. California*, the Court had to decide whether a trial court's admission of expert testimony about the alcoholic content of a citizen-defendant's blood violated his Fifth Amendment privilege against self-incrimination: chiefly because a policeman had ordered the medical staff to withdraw the blood contrary to the citizen-defendant's objection. Declaring that the privilege did not apply in this situation, the Court held that the privilege protects an accused only from being compelled to testify about his own acts, or where it would otherwise provide the state with evidence of a testimonial or communicative nature.

In addition, the Court noted that it had previously ruled in 1910 that witness testimony at trial describing the defendant's act of putting on and wearing a blouse (that fit him) did not amount to testimonial evidence. Since *Schmerber*, the Court has consistently held that a defendant is not compelled to offer testimonial evidence when he is compelled to display his body or otherwise present physical attributes of himself. The Court has concluded that a defendant also does not offer testimonial evidence when he (1) supplies a handwriting sample used at trial, (2) provides a voice exemplar to a grand jury, (3) appears at a pretrial lineup and speaks words made by the alleged robber, or (4) signs, pursuant to a court order, forms consenting to disclosure of his bank records. Indeed, the Court has emphasized that in order to be testimonial an accused's communication must itself, explicitly or implicitly, relate to a factual assertion or disclose information.

Limits on the Fifth Amendment Privilege

In *New Jersey v. Portash*, the Court recognized that the use of a citizen's immunized grand jury testimony against him in a criminal prosecution violated his Fifth Amendment right against compelled self-incrimination because testimony given in response to a grant of legislative immunity is the essence of coerced testimony.

Although the Court appears to preclude the use of immunized testimony against the accused for any purpose, the Court has allowed immunized testimony to be used to prosecute a citizen for making false statements under a federal immunity statute, 18 U.S.C. § 6002. Similarly, the Court has held that if a testifying witness makes a false statement in violation of 18 U.S.C. § 1001, that it will not recognize the so-called *exculpatory no* doctrine as an exception to a violation of the statute. The *exculpatory no* doctrine, which had been adopted by some federal circuits, excused a simple denial of guilt, even if false, from coming within the statute. Essentially, the Court reasoned that falsely denying guilt in a government investigation violates an objective of the statute: criminalizing the perversion of a governmental function.

A Person or a Corporation Who May Invoke

Although the Court has recently deemed corporations persons under the First Amendment, the Court has reached an opposite conclusion under the Fifth Amendment. As early as 1906, in *Hale v. Henkel*, the Court emphatically held that a corporation was not a person within the meaning of the Fifth Amendment. Primarily, the Court concluded that the right of a person under the Fifth Amendment to refuse to incriminate himself is purely a personal privilege of the witness. As a consequence, the Fifth Amendment is limited to a person who shall be compelled in any criminal case to be a witness against himself, and if he cannot set up the privilege of a third person, he certainly cannot set up the privilege of a corporation.

However, even a person's right to invoke the privilege has been limited by the Court where the government compels a citizen to produce information pursuant to a required records law, and the records are to be used under a noncriminal regulatory scheme. In *Shapiro v. United States*, the defendant invoked his Fifth Amendment privilege in refusing to disclose records demanded by a government subpoena under the Emergency Price Control Act. By invoking the privilege, the defendant attempted to secure the protection of the immunity provision in the act that accompanied the privilege. The Court held that the defendant could not invoke the privilege because the act did not extend the immunity from prosecution to him.

On the other hand, the Court has opined that a citizen should be aware that the act of producing the document or thing may have Fifth Amendment implications. For example, in *Fisher v. United States*, the Court had to decide whether the Fifth Amendment privilege was implicated where the Internal Revenue Service (IRS) summons sought the work papers of a tax payer's accountant, which were being held by the taxpayer's attorney. The Court stated that a taxpayer may not avoid compliance with an IRS summons merely because the requested documents contained incriminating evidence. Indeed, the Court concluded that the Fifth Amendment privilege applies only when the accused is compelled to make a testimonial communication that is incriminating. Here, the Court determined that compelling the taxpayer to produce his accountant's work papers involved substantial compulsion, but it did not compel oral testimony.

Nevertheless, the Court has held that a citizen may not invoke the privilege even if the act of producing evidence in response to a subpoena under the facts and circumstances of particular cases may be both testimonial and incriminating. In other words, the act of producing the documents tacitly admits their existence and their location in the hands of their possessor. The Court has held in *Baltimore City Department of Social Services v. Bouknight* that even if the act of producing a child amounted to testimony showing a citizen's control over and possession of the child, the Fifth Amendment privilege was not implicated. In *Bouknight*, a mother was required by court order, despite her Fifth Amendment objection, to produce her previously abused child over whom she had been granted custody by the court. Although the Court acknowledged that the mother's act of producing the child was a limited testimonial assertion, which in turn was sufficiently incriminating and sufficiently testimonial for purposes of the privilege, the Court held that the mother may not invoke the privilege to resist the production order because she had assumed custodial duties related to production, under a required noncriminal regulatory regime.

HYPOTHETICAL

Police Chief Marck Jackson (hereafter "Chief Jackson") of the Fayetteberg Police Department found the following anonymous letter under his office door around 7:30 am on May 29, 2004:

> I am an employee at Wal-Market Super Center on 12th Street in Fayetteberg. You should know that several people on the Wal-Market management staff at this store are selling powdered cocaine to kids at Fayetteberg High School and Romney Jr. High. Two kids at Romney Jr. High died from overdosing on this toxic dope. The street name of this cocaine is "Triple H."
>
> By the way, some of these Wal-Market managers are quite well-known in the community. Two of them are named "Bob." You know them well! They brag on how they've made so much money selling drugs and how they can hide it through their regular jobs. *Some of the invoices for Wal-*Market products have been commingled with records from drug sales. They sell the cocaine from the employee restrooms at the 12th Street store. They usually sell it as *"8 balls"*—at $250 per "8 ball." They also use the employee lockers to store (and sometimes sell from) the drugs. The drugs are sometimes stored in their cars.

Chief Jackson conducted a search of police files to determine if any students from Romney Jr. High had recently died of toxic drugs. After a two-hour search, he found records of three recent deaths by toxic drugs. Two of these deaths were of seventh graders at Canal Jr. High. The other death was of an eighth grader at Romney Jr. High. He also had several tips from reliable informants that "Bob" Sample sold drugs in the neighborhood.

After this search, Chief Jackson called the Wal-Market Home Office in Collierville. Chief Jackson identified himself and asked the appropriate personnel to locate the full name and address of the manager, "Jim Bob," at the 12th Street Super Center. After a ninety-minute search, the Home Office confirmed that there were two employee-managers at that store named "Bob." "Jim Bob" Sample was not only in his seventh year as a manager, but he was also a popular country-western singer in the Ozarks; and James Robert ("Bob") Powell was a two-year veteran and a popular thespian in a local theater troupe. "Bob" Powell, however, was on duty at a Wal-Market in China. So Chief Jackson had a subpoena duces team served on Wal-Market Manager Bob Sample. The subpoena was limited to those records required to be maintained under federal and state law at that store. Thus, the scope of the subpoena (for that store) was limited to federal and state tax returns, W-2 forms, unemployment and Worker's Compensation records, and purchase/sales agreements under state law.

Sample has moved to quash the subpoena on the grounds that the act of production would involve compelled self-incrimination because he is the sole manager of this 12th Street Wal-Market Store.

Defendant has filed a Motion to Quash Prosecutor's Subpoena Duces Team. You are an associate prosecutor. Please provide your senior prosecutor with a memorandum of law: (1) analyzing the key legal precedents that the defendant will likely use to support his motions, (2) isolating the most persuasive arguments distilled from those precedents, and (3) predicting how the court is likely to rule on these competing arguments.

LIST OF READINGS

1. The Fifth Amendment to the United States Constitution.
2. Federal Rules of Evidence Rule 401. Definition of Relevant Evidence.
3. Federal Rules of Evidence Rule 402. Relevant Evidence Generally Admissible; Irrelevant Evidence Inadmissible.
4. *Brown v. Walker,* 161 U.S. 591 (1896).
5. *Lefkowitz v. Turley*, 414 U.S. 70 (1973).
6. *Counselman v. Hitchcock*, 142 U.S. 547 (1892).
7. *Kastigar v. United States*, 406 U.S. 441 (1972).
8. *Doe v. United States*, 487 U.S. 201 (1988).
9. *United States v. Apfelbaum*, 445 U.S. 115 (1980).
10. *Hale v. Henkel*, 201 U.S. 43 (1906).
11. *Shapiro v. United States*, 335 U.S. 1 (1948).
12. *Baltimore City Department of Social Services*, 493 U.S. 549 (1990).
13. *New Jersey v. Portash*, 440 U.S. 450 (1979).

SAMPLE ESSAY

To: Senior Prosecutor
From: Associate Prosecutor
Re: Suppression Hearing—[*State v. Sample*]
Defendant's Motions to Quash Prosecutor's Subpoena Duces Team
Date:

In anticipation of the forthcoming Motion to Quash the Prosecutor's Subpoena *Duces Team* by the defendant, I have prepared the following memorandum of law for your consideration. As you will discover, this memorandum attempts to (1) identify the key legal precedents that the defendant will use to support his Motion under the facts set out below, (2) isolate the most persuasive arguments distilled from these precedents that he is likely to assert (and our counterarguments to them), and (3) predict how the court is likely to rule on these competing arguments.

Essentially, the defendant will argue that because he is the sole manager/proprietor of the Wal-Market 12th Street Store, the government subpoena demanding that he produce the store's business records was, in fact, a demand for his personal records. He will claim that the United States Supreme Court has held that a sole proprietor is entitled to Fifth Amendment protection. Moreover, he will contend that the act of producing the business documents is also accorded Fifth Amendment protection. Neither one of these arguments should support the Fifth Amendment shielding these documents from disclosure.

First, the Court has emphasized that the Fifth Amendment privilege is limited to a person, and that a citizen cannot set up the privilege of a corporation. Because the defendant's store reports to a corporate headquarters, it is doubtful that he could successfully show that he was a sole proprietor. In fact, the leading case supporting Fifth Amendment protection for a sole proprietor, unlike the bare assertion in our facts, noted that there was no question that the respondent was the owner of several sole proprietorships.

Second, a defendant cannot secure protection from disclosure under the Fifth Amendment merely because the requested documents contain incriminating evidence. Additionally, the Court has noted that the Fifth Amendment applies only where the citizen is compelled to make a testimonial communication.

Third, it is true, as the defendant will argue, that the Court has recognized that the act of producing documents may involve testimonial incrimination. However, where the Court found that the act of producing documents implicated the Fifth Amendment privilege, the Court reached that conclusion because it had the explicit finding of the district court that the act of producing the documents would involve testimonial self-incrimination. There is no comparable finding under our facts.

Fourth, the Court has held that a custodian of corporate records may not claim the Fifth Amendment privilege.

TOOLS FOR SELF-CRITICISM

The issues to be determined under our hypothetical were whether the defendant could successfully invoke the Fifth Amendment privilege in order to quash subpoenas seeking corporate documents in his possession on the theory that he was either a sole proprietor or that his act of producing the documents would involve testimonial self-incrimination. On our facts, the Fifth Amendment self-incrimination privilege does not apply to either situation. The Court has emphasized that in order to be testimonial an accused's communication must itself, explicitly or implicitly, relate to a factual assertion or disclose information.

VARIATIONS ON A THEME

Try the same problem, but this time the subpoena was not limited to those records required to be maintained under federal and state law at that store, but it also included any personal records that Bob Sample left at the store. Does this change the result?

CONFESSIONS AND INTERROGATIONS

10

OPENING REMARKS

The United States Supreme Court has held that the Fifth Amendment and the due process clause of the Fourteenth Amendment preclude admitting involuntary confession in federal and state criminal cases respectively. That is, only a voluntary confession is admissible. Like its Fifth Amendment counterpart, the due process voluntariness test protects a citizen only against official action. In addition to this threshold requirement, the Court has developed several analytical markers to its due process voluntariness test.

The Supreme Court has held that a trial court must determine the voluntariness of a confession before the jury considers it on the question of guilt or innocence. On the other hand, the Court has held that it is a denial of procedural fairness for a trial court to preclude a defendant from introducing testimony about the environment in which the police secured his confession, even if it has determined that the confession was voluntary. Such evidence, opined the Court, is especially relevant where there is no other physical evidence to link the defendant to the crime.

Similarly, the Court has held that a citizen's Fourteenth Amendment due process rights were violated or his confession involuntary when the citizen confessed after (1) brutal beatings by the police; (2) thirty-six consecutive hours of police questioning; (3) after indictment, multiple interrogators questioning him over an extended period of time and the citizen's repeated refusal to answer on the advice of counsel; (4) the chief of police telling him that "he would probably keep" a mob of thirty to forty people from coming inside the jail facility to get the citizen if he confessed; and (5) an undercover informant posing as a fellow inmate in a federal correctional facility making a "credible threat of physical violence" unless the inmate confessed. Because the facts supporting the voluntariness of a confession varied so widely, predicting the outcome of admissibility was problematic. The Court sought a more consistent standard for determining the admissibility of confessions.

Miranda v. Arizona

The seminal opinion of *Miranda v. Arizona* is comprised of four consolidated cases. The *Miranda* Court addressed an issue it had considered two years earlier in *Escobedo v. Illinois*: whether statements are admissible in Court if they are obtained from an individual who was subjected to custodial police interrogation without the procedures that assure that he was accorded his privilege under the Fifth Amendment to the Constitution not to be compelled to incriminate himself. By holding that the statements obtained in each of the four cases must be excluded, the Court opined that exclusion was (1) an effective way to enforce the constitutional rights of the individual against overzealous police practices, and (2) consistent with the spirit, principles, and holding in *Escobedo*.

The *Miranda* Court noted that the constitutional issue to be decided in each of the cases was the admissibility of statements obtained from a defendant questioned while in custody but who had not been given a full and effective warning of his rights at the outset of the interrogation process. Accordingly, the Court granted certiorari in order to determine how to apply the privilege against self-incrimination to in-custody interrogations. In brief, the Court held that the prosecution may not use statements, whether exculpatory or inculpatory, stemming from custodial interrogation of the defendant unless it uses effective procedural safeguards to secure the privilege against self-incrimination. The required procedural safeguards consisted of a precise incantation, which was to be delivered prior to any questioning. This precise incantation comprised the familiar *Miranda* warnings. The person must be warned that he has a right to remain silent, that any statement he does make may be used as evidence against him, and that he has a right to the presence of an attorney, either retained or appointed.

Nevertheless, a citizen may waive these rights provided the waiver is made voluntarily, knowingly, and intelligently. In any event, at this first level of *Miranda*'s protections, a citizen must be given a full and effective warning of his rights at the outset of the interrogation process if the prosecutor plans to use the statements (as evidence at trial) made by that citizen during that custodial interrogation.

Miranda provides a second level of protection. At this second level, the police are required to honor (by ceasing the interrogation) the decision of a citizen who indicates in *any manner* that he wishes to consult with an attorney before speaking to the police, or who states that he wishes not to be interrogated. Indeed, the police are precluded from interrogating a citizen even if he failed to express that wish not to be interrogated until after he had already answered some questions or volunteered some statements. Although *Miranda* appears to have clearly identified and defined the requirements in both levels, subsequent interpretations by the Court have not, to say the least, adhered to the original formulations. What follows is a list of some of the Court's reinterpretations of *Miranda*'s key principles.

Miranda's View of Custody

The *Miranda* Court defined "in-custody" broadly as a citizen being otherwise deprived (by a government agent) of his freedom of action in any significant way. The Court opined that a citizen was in-custody if he was swept from familiar surroundings into police custody or if he was in the isolated setting of the police station.

The Court's Subsequent Interpretations—of Custody

Initially, the Court followed this broad interpretation when it held that a citizen was deemed in-custody for *Miranda* purposes, even though he was interrogated on his own bed and in familiar surroundings, primarily because the Court noted that the interrogating officer testified that the defendant was under arrest when he was interrogated. Since that time, however, the Court has defined in-custody more narrowly. For example, the Court has held that a probationer was not in-custody for *Miranda* purposes because there was no formal arrest or restraint of movement to the degree associated with a formal arrest. The Court also concluded that an interview of a probationer arranged by appointment at a mutually convenient time would not convey to a probationer that he was under custodial arrest. Besides, the Court observed that the probationer's regular meetings with his probation officer should have served to familiarize him with her and her office in order to insulate him from psychological intimidation.

Custody and the Prison Inmate

In 1968, the Court held that a prison inmate serving a state prison sentence was in-custody when he was interrogated by a Federal Internal Revenue Service agent. However, twenty-two years later the Court held that the mere fact of incarceration does not necessarily mean that an inmate was in-custody during a police interrogation. In this latter case, the Court reasoned that when an inmate does not know he is talking to a government agent, there is no reason to assume the possibility that the suspect might feel coerced.

In 2012, the Court narrowed in-custody even more for a prison inmate. There, a state prisoner was escorted from his prison cell to a conference room where he was interrogated about criminal activity that he allegedly engaged in prior to the crime that sent him to prison. Although the inmate was questioned for many hours, the interrogating officers never gave him *Miranda* warnings. Even so, the Court concluded that his *Miranda* rights were not violated because the inmate was not in-custody for *Miranda* purposes on account of all the circumstances of the questioning, especially as the respondent was told that he was free to end the questioning and that he could return to his cell. Accounting for all the circumstances in the context of *Miranda* sounds eerily like the voluntariness test.

Custody in Miscellaneous Contexts

A citizen is not in-custody during a routine traffic stop. Nor is a citizen in-custody during a *Terry* stop (*Terry* stop is explained in Chapter 7). And, a citizen is not in-custody when the citizen is not under restraint and the police subject him to general on-the-scene questioning as to the facts surrounding a crime, or other general questioning regarding the fact-finding process.

What Is an Interrogation

Another element in *Miranda*'s first level of protection is custodial interrogation. Custodial interrogation was defined in *Miranda* as questioning initiated by law enforcement officers after a person has been taken into custody or otherwise deprived of his freedom of action in any significant way. From police manuals, the Court concluded that the principal psychological factor contributing to a successful interrogation is privacy: being alone with the person under interrogation. This psychological stratagem, noted the Court, may include express questioning, trickery, or deception. Hence, *Miranda* was not limited to express questioning.

The Court's Subsequent Interpretations of Interrogation

Since the Court's decision in *Miranda*, it has acknowledged that the starting point for defining interrogation is found in that seminal opinion. Still, the Court has subsequently held that the *Miranda* safeguards come into play whenever a person in custody is subjected to either express questioning or its functional equivalent. A functional equivalent interrogation means any words or actions on the part of the police (other than those normally attendant to arrest and custody) that the police should know are reasonably likely to elicit an incriminating response. As this definition focuses primarily upon the perceptions of the suspect, rather than the intent of the police, the Court emphasized that any knowledge the police may have had concerning the unusual susceptibility of a defendant to a particular form of persuasion might be an important factor in determining whether the police should have known that their words or actions were reasonably likely to elicit an incriminating response from the suspect. On the other hand, the intent of the police may be relevant because it may bear on whether the police should have known that their words or actions were reasonably likely to evoke an incriminating response.

Interrogation during the Booking Process—An Exception to Interrogation

The Court has held that a citizen's answers to questions posed by the police at the police station during the *booking* process were admissible because the questions fell within a routine "booking question" exception. This booking exception exempts from *Miranda*'s coverage questions to secure the biographical data necessary to complete an arrestee's booking or pretrial services. However, a citizen's answer is not admissible when it is the fruit of a *Miranda* violation. For example, if the booking officer, without providing the familiar warnings, poses a personal question (what was the date of your sixth birthday?) that elicits a testimonial response, *Miranda* is violated.

What Are the Familiar Warnings?

At *Miranda*'s first level of protection a prosecutor who plans to use the exculpatory or inculpatory statement stemming from a custodial interrogation of a suspect must demonstrate that he used procedural safeguards effective to secure the citizen's privilege against self-incrimination. The *Miranda* Court emphasized that a precise incantation was required for its procedural safeguards. The Court required this precise incantation unless the police could show that other effective means created by Congress or the states were used.

Is a Precise Incantation of the Warnings Required?

Although *Miranda* encouraged Congress and the states to devise other fully effective means, instead, alternatives have been developed exclusively by the police (and sanctioned by the Court) misreading how other fully effective warnings may be created. The Court has held that *Miranda* warnings are adequate even if the police do not fully convey them. Indeed, the police need only *reasonably convey* a citizen's rights. For example, *Miranda* warnings are not inadequate merely because a citizen was advised that counsel would be appointed "if and when you go to court." The warnings were held adequate because the warnings reasonably conveyed his rights as required by *Miranda*.

Similarly, the Court has held that the failure by the police to expressly advise a citizen of the right to the presence of counsel during questioning did not result in inadequate warnings because the combination of informing a citizen of the right to consult a lawyer before answering any question, plus the warning that he had the right to use any of his rights at any time during the interview, resulted in those two warnings reasonably conveying the right to have an attorney present during questioning.

Is a Precise Incantation of the Warnings Necessarily Adequate?

The Court has cautioned that "just as 'no talismanic incantation is required to satisfy *Miranda*'s strictures; it would be absurd to think that mere recitation of the familiar warnings' litany suffice to satisfy *Miranda* in every conceivable circumstance." The inquiry is simply whether the warnings reasonably convey to a suspect the rights required by *Miranda*. For example, the Court held in *Missouri v. Seibert* that *Miranda*'s familiar warnings may not be effectively conveyed in a two-step, question-first/later-warned interrogation technique. In this instance, the technique was to withhold the warnings until after the unwarned interrogation had succeeded in soliciting a confession. The Court concluded that the subsequent warnings would be ineffective in preparing the interrogated citizen for a successive interrogation, close in time and similar in content to the unwarned interrogation. The Court concluded that the facts of *Seibert* showed that the question-first (or unwarned) interrogation was conducted in a systematic and exhaustive manner at the station house. Moreover, the Court stated that at the conclusion of this unwarned interrogation, there was little, if anything of incriminating potential left unsaid. So, the subsequent warned interrogation was merely a continuation of the unwarned session. However, the Court reached a different result in *Oregon v. Elstad* even though based on a similar set of facts. In *Elstad* where the Court described the arresting officer's failure to give *Miranda* warnings at the question-first (unwarned) phase as possibly the result of confusion as to whether the brief exchange with the suspect qualified as a custodial interrogation, *Miranda* did not appear to apply. As the Court concluded that none of the earmarks of coercion appeared during the brief question-first phase, the suspect's confession at the subsequent warned phase was voluntary because the *Miranda* warnings were effectively conveyed at this markedly different subsequent phase.

In another case, *Warden v. Dixon,* where the police conducted a deliberate "question-first" interrogation, the defendant gave a full confession by placing most of the blame on his confederate. Although the defendant's confession was the product of a deliberate question-first/warn later strategy, the Court in *Warden v. Dixon* held that the break in time and the dramatic change in circumstances created a new and distinct experience, ensuring that the defendant's prior unwarned interrogation did not undermine the effectiveness of the *Miranda* warnings he received before confessing to the murder at the second or subsequent interrogation.

When Are the Miranda Warnings Not Required?

Soon after *Miranda* was decided, the Court concluded and announced that the *warnings* were not (themselves) rights protected by the Fifth Amendment; instead they were prophylactic rules designed to protect the Fifth Amendment right against self-incrimination. For example, the Court held that a police officer's failure to give full *Miranda* warnings did not violate a citizen's constitutional privilege against compulsory self-incrimination. According to the Court, as this failure was merely a violation of a prophylactic, the testimony of a third-party witness was admissible at trial even through the third-party was identified by the incriminating statements that were the fruits of this violation. In a similar way, the Court has held that a police officer's failure to read the familiar warnings to a citizen-suspect prior to a custodial interrogation could not be used as the necessary constitutional violation in order to support a 42 U.S.C. § 1983 federal civil claim for damages against the police.

The Court has also held that a policeman may withhold providing a citizen with the familiar warnings where on the facts there is a public safety exception demanding that the police locate and secure a dangerous gun. Similarly, the Court has concluded that a failure to give *Miranda* warnings did not require the suppression of the physical fruits of a suspect's unwarned, but voluntary statements.

Although the Court continues (somehow) to adhere to the principle that *Miranda* is both a prophylactic (because it is not based on the Constitution), it has also held that *Miranda* was a constitutional rule that Congress may not supercede legislatively. Stay tuned.

Impeaching the Defendant's Credibility with Fruits from a *Miranda* Violation

In a case where a defendant was charged with selling drugs to an undercover police officer, the defendant later testified at trial that he did not sell drugs to anyone. Moreover, the defendant specifically asserted that he had not sold drugs on the particular day identified in the charging instrument. However, on cross-examination the prosecutor asked the defendant, among other things,

> Whether he had made specified statements to the police *immediately following* his arrest, statements that partially contradicted petitioner's direct testimony at trial.

The United States Supreme Court held that the fruits of a *Miranda* violation could be used (in this way) by the prosecutor to impeach the credibility of a testifying defendant because

> Having voluntarily taken the stand, petitioner was under an obligation to speak truthfully and accurately, and the prosecution here did no more than utilize the traditional truth-testing devices of the adversary process.

In other words, explained the Court, *Miranda* could not be used to commit perjury, free from the risk of confrontation with prior inconsistent utterances. The Court has allowed this impeachment exception to *Miranda* even where the police violated the citizen's express request for an attorney.

Impeaching the Defendant's Credibility with Silence

Although the Court has opined that it is true that *Miranda* warnings contain no express assurance that silence will carry no penalty, the Court has held that it would be fundamentally unfair and a deprivation of due process to use a citizen's post-*Miranda* warnings silence to impeach him. On the other hand, a prosecutor may use a citizen's pre-arrest silence to impeach.

Waiving Miranda Rights

Miranda held, among other things, that a citizen may waive effectuation of these rights provided the waiver is made voluntarily, knowingly, and intelligently. At another juncture in the opinion, the Court stated that

> If the interrogation continues without the presence of an attorney and a statement is taken, a *heavy burden* rests on the government to demonstrate that the defendant

> knowingly and intelligently waived his privilege against self-incrimination and his right to retained or appointed counsel.

In any event, the Court has determined that waivers of counsel must not only be voluntary, but must also constitute a knowing and intelligent relinquishment or abandonment of a known right or privilege. Still, the Court has held that an *express* waiver is not required. Indeed, a citizen may *implicitly* waive his *Miranda* rights. For example, the Court has concluded that a defendant's silence, coupled with an understanding of his rights and a course of conduct, may constitute a waiver of rights. Moreover, the Court emphasized that

> The question of waiver, must be determined on the particular facts and circumstances surrounding that case, including the background, experience, and conduct of the accused.

Miranda's Second Level—Invoking Silence or Counsel

Once the police have a citizen in-custody and have precisely or reasonably conveyed *Miranda*'s familiar warnings at its *first level*, the citizen may cut off further interrogation at *Miranda*'s *second level* by indicating in any manner that he wishes to consult with an attorney before speaking to the police, or that he wishes not to be interrogated. Whether invoking silence or counsel, *Miranda* allowed a citizen to invoke (the right to silence or counsel) *in any manner*.

Is Invokingin *Any Manner* Sufficient?

Since *Miranda*, the Court has opined that a request for (invoking the right to) counsel pursuant to *Miranda*'s prophylactic rule requires a more precisely articulated invocation. As a consequence, the Court has concluded that to avoid difficulties of proof and to provide guidance to police officers conducting interrogations, determining the sufficiency of a request for counsel is an objective inquiry. That is, a citizen must unambiguously request counsel or unambiguously invoke the right to remain silent. Moreover, a citizen fails to invoke by persistently remaining silent for several hours.

> he must articulate his desire to have counsel present sufficiently clearly that a reasonable police officer in the circumstances would understand the statement to be a request for an attorney.

Likewise, an invocation of the right to remain silent must be done unambiguously. If it is unclear to the officer ("I probably should speak with a lawyer") whether the citizen has invoked silence or requested counsel, the officer may continue the interrogation.

Moreover, the Court has recently held in *Salinas v. Texas* that a citizen may not invoke silence by merely remaining silent during most of the interrogation session. In *Salinas*, the citizen-suspect was interrogated by the police during a noncustodial session. That is, no *Miranda* warnings were required or given. Even so, the citizen-suspect declined to answer any questions (except for a few "yes" or "no" responses) for two hours. However, a few of his "yes" or "no" responses proved fatal. As a result, the Court held that the prosecutor could comment on how the citizen-suspect reacted when he was asked whether he thought the shotgun shells found at a murder scene would fit his shotgun. According to the Court, a citizen could not invoke silence by merely remaining silent; he must specifically invoke it.

Similarly, in *Berghuis v. Thompkins*, the Court held that a citizen did not invoke silence because he refused to sign a waiver-of-rights form or because he chose not to respond to most of the police interrogator's questions. Indeed, because the citizen-suspect failed to specifically invoke silence, the prosecutor's witness (interrogating police officer) was allowed to testify that the citizen suspect answered yes to a series of questions that implied he committed the criminal act:

> *"Do you believe in God?"*
> *"Do you pray to God?"*
> *"Do you pray that God will forgive you for shooting that boy down?"*

Invoking the Right to Silence—*Michigan v. Mosley*

According to *Miranda*, when a citizen indicates *in any manner* that he wishes to remain silent the subsequent procedure is clear: the interrogation must cease. However, *Miranda* failed to make clear whether or under what circumstances a police interrogator may resume questioning. Nearly ten years after *Miranda*, the Court answered this query with a two-step rule.

First, the police interrogator must scrupulously honor the citizen's invocation by immediately ceasing to question him. Second, the police may resume questioning only (1) after the passage of a significant period of time (at least two hours), (2) where they provide a fresh set of warnings, and (3) where the second interrogation is restricted to a crime that had not been a subject of the earlier interrogation.

Invoking the Right to Counsel—*Edwards v. Arizona*

In addition to requiring that a citizen must unambiguously request counsel, the Court has also emphasized that

> When an accused has invoked his right to have counsel present during custodial interrogation… a valid waiver of that right cannot be established by showing only that he responded to further police initiated custodial interrogation… until counsel has been made available to him unless the accused himself initiates further communication, exchanges, or conversations with the police.

Similarly, a citizen-suspect who has invoked the right to counsel cannot be (further) questioned regarding *any* offense unless an attorney is actually present or the citizen initiates the discussion with the police. A subsequent interrogation without counsel is prohibited pursuant to *Edwards*, where the citizen-suspect requested and then consulted with counsel.

The Court has opined that the rationale of *Edwards* is that once the citizen-suspect has invoked the right to counsel, he has declared that he is not capable of undergoing custodial questioning without the advice of counsel. Hence, any *custodial* interrogation after his invocation would be the product of inherently compelling pressures. However, the *Edwards* prophylactic rule against subsequent custodial interrogations (without counsel) does not apply if there was a *break in custody*. Consequently, once the citizen has invoked the right to counsel (*Edwards*) and he has returned to normal life for some time before the later attempted interrogations, the Court has concluded that there is little reason to think that the statements were coerced. Even a state prison inmate was *not* in *Miranda* custody where the subsequent interrogation occurred after he was returned to the general prison population.

The Court also determined what it meant by the duration of the *break in custody* or what it means for someone to have returned to his normal life for *some time* before the later attempted interrogation. There has been a *break in custody* if the citizen has returned to his normal life for fourteen days (some time) before the later attempted interrogation. If so, the *Edwards* prohibition does not preclude the later interrogation (post-*Miranda* warnings).

The *Edwards* prohibition against subjecting a citizen, who has invoked counsel, to further interrogation does not apply where the citizen has *initiated* a desire for a generalized discussion about the investigation. In other words, cautioned the Court, the *Edwards* prohibition does not apply where the citizen *initiated* a conversation about something *other than* a necessary inquiry arising out of the incidents of the custodial relationship ("May I use the restroom now (?)"). Regrettably, the *Miranda-Edwards* Fifth Amendment right to counsel has been confused with the Sixth Amendment right to counsel. What follows is a brief description of the Court's treatment of (1) the Sixth Amendment right to counsel, (2) the combination of the Fifth Amendment and Sixth Amendment right to counsel, and (3) the resolution of the confusion in this combination.

The Sixth Amendment Right to Counsel and Confessions

The Sixth Amendment to the United States Constitution guarantees a criminal defendant the right to have the assistance of counsel for his defense. The Court has limited the language: "Assistance of Counsel for... defense" to "[i]n all criminal prosecutions." Therefore the protections of the Sixth Amendment attach automatically if formal proceedings (indictment, arraignment, etc.) have been commenced against a citizen. It is only when such proceedings are initiated that a government has committed itself to prosecute, and only then have the adverse positions of government and defendant solidified. So, the Court has stated that the right to counsel granted by the Sixth Amendment means, at least, that a person is entitled to the help of a lawyer at or after the time judicial proceedings have been initiated against him.

The Court held in *Massiah v. United States* that a citizen was denied the basic protections of the Sixth Amendment guarantee when there was used against him at his trial evidence of his own incriminating words, which federal agents had deliberately (and surreptitiously) elicited from him, in the absence of counsel, after he had been indicted. Following *Massiah*, the Court held in *United States v. Henry* that the government violated the Sixth Amendment right to counsel post-indictment when it created a situation likely to induce the defendant to make incriminating statements without the assistance of counsel. The government created a situation likely to induce incriminating statements by employing an jail-inmate post-indictment as an undercover informant to pose as the defendant's fellow-inmate.

Similarly, the Court has held in *Maine v. Moulton* that the defendant's Sixth Amendment rights were violated even though the defendant instigated the meeting with his alleged accomplice who was, in turn, serving as an undercover informant.

According to the Court, "who instigated the meeting... was not decisive or even important" to its decision in *Massiah*. The Court emphasized the following:

> The Sixth Amendment guarantees the accused, at least after the initiation of formal charges, the right to rely on counsel as a medium between him and the State. This guarantee includes the State's affirmative obligation not to act in a manner that circumvents the protections accorded the accused by invoking this right.

Based on these opinions, the Court appeared to emphasize that the key to determine whether the government had violated the Sixth Amendment, was whether its agents deliberately acted in a manner that circumvented the protections of the Sixth Amendment. Once a citizen's Sixth Amendment rights have attached (after formal proceedings have commenced), even if the government merely arranges to record the conversations between the defendant and the informant, a Sixth Amendment violation has occurred. If this was the Court's interpretation at one time, it is no longer the basic understanding.

Since those decisions, the Court held in *Kuhlman v. Wilson* that a Sixth Amendment violation has not occurred if the defendant cannot show that the police or their (undercover) jail informant took some action beyond merely listening (to the defendant) that was designed deliberately to elicit incriminating remarks. Hence, even in a post-formal proceedings environment (where the right to counsel has attached), the government's undercover informant (at least in a jail environment) must encourage the defendant to speak, in order for the action to constitute "deliberately eliciting."

Waiving *Massiah*'s Sixth Amendment Right to Counsel (Confused with *Miranda*'s Fifth Amendment Right to Counsel)

In *Michigan v. Jackson*, the Supreme Court adopted a *non-waiver* rule. A citizen could not waive his Sixth Amendment right to counsel, the Court held, if the citizen had requested appointed counsel at his arraignment and the purported waiver occurs before he has consulted counsel. The state had argued that the defendant had waived both his *Miranda-Edwards* and his Sixth Amendment rights to counsel because he had failed to invoke *Miranda-Edwards* right to counsel after receiving *Miranda* warnings at his post- arraignment custodial interrogation session. Besides, the state argued that the *Miranda-Edwards* right to counsel was different from the automatic Sixth Amendment right to counsel; the Court rejected the state's arguments.

The *Jackson* Court explained that this citizen's post-arraignment right to counsel had two sources: *Miranda-Edwards* Fifth Amendment and the Sixth Amendment. These two sources of the right to counsel meant that an uncounseled prisoner who has requested the help of a lawyer at a formal proceeding (arraignment) could not be subsequently interrogated even if the police provided *Miranda* warnings and even though the citizen failed to invoke counsel. In essence, the Court opined that the citizen could not be interrogated, because he had invoked *Miranda-Edwards* right to counsel at the arraignment (formal proceedings). As the interrogation was prohibited, the citizen could not waive his rights (non-waiver rule).

The Court has, however, overruled *Michigan v. Jackson* and restored (I think) the distinction between the *Miranda-Edwards* right to counsel (where a citizen is required to unambiguously invoke counsel) versus the Sixth Amendment right to counsel (where the right to counsel attaches automatically at the onset of formal proceedings).

First, in *McNeil v. Wisconsin*, the Court held that the Sixth Amendment right to counsel is offense specific. For example, if a citizen is arraigned on a *robbery* charge, his Sixth Amendment right to counsel automatically attaches to that charge. If subsequent to this formal charge he is *Mirandized* and subjected to custodial interrogation about a *murder*, his Sixth Amendment right to counsel does not apply to the interrogation for murder. Neither is his *Miranda-Edwards* Fifth Amendment right to counsel implicated if he fails to unambiguously request counsel.

Second, in *Texas v. Cobb,* the Court held that even if a citizen-suspect is formally charged with only one of several factually related crimes, he may claim a Sixth Amendment right only as to the formally charged offense. However, *Cobb* does provide that the citizen-suspect may be able to claim a Sixth Amendment right regarding the uncharged factually related offenses if he can show that those offenses require the same elements of proof as the charged offense.

Third, in *Montejo v. Louisiana*, the Court specifically overruled *Michigan v. Jackson's* non-waiver rule. Among other things, the *Montejo* Court held that a citizen-suspect may not invoke the *Miranda-Edwards* right to counsel at arraignment proceedings or in advance of the post-arraignment custodial interrogation. More important, once the citizen-suspect receives the *Miranda* warnings, he may, by failing to unambiguously invoke *Miranda-Edwards*, waive both his *Miranda-Edwards* right to counsel and his Sixth Amendment right to counsel (at least at that post-arraignment custodial-interrogation session).

Exceptions to the Court's Sixth Amendment Exclusionary Rule

The United States Supreme Court's Sixth Amendment exclusionary rule precludes the use of a citizen's incriminating words at trial when federal agents have deliberately (and surreptitiously) elicited those words in the absence of counsel, after that citizen was formally charged. Still, even where incriminating statements were the fruits of a Sixth Amendment violation, they are not subject to exclusion if they could have been secured pursuant to either *inevitable* or *independent* discovery.

INEVITABLE DISCOVERY

In the leading case (*Nix v. Williams*) defining *inevitable* discovery, the police questioned a citizen-defendant concerning the whereabouts of a murder victim, after he had been arraigned and outside the presence of his lawyer, in violation of the Sixth Amendment. The citizen-defendant agreed to show his police questioners where the body could be found. And, he took them to that place. At trial, the citizen-defendant argued that the evidence relating to the location and existence of the victim's body could not be admitted against him because it was a fruit of a Sixth Amendment violation. The prosecutor's rebuttal was that although the police had violated the defendant's right to counsel, evidence concerning the location of the victim's body was admissible because it inevitably would have been found by search groups who were approaching the actual location of the body at the time that the Sixth Amendment violation occurred.

Because the Court agreed with the theory of inevitable discovery, it concluded that the prosecutor should not be put in a *worse* position simply because of some earlier police error, and that the prosecutor had satisfied the applicable test for proving *inevitable* discovery.

> If the government can prove that the evidence would have been obtained inevitably and, therefore, would have been admitted regardless of any overreaching by the police, there is no rational basis to keep that evidence from the jury in order to ensure the fairness of the trial proceedings.

As a consequence, the Court concluded that it was clear that because the search parties were approaching the actual location of the body, the police would have inevitably discovered it.

INDEPENDENT DISCOVERY

Unlike the inevitable discovery doctrine, the independent discovery doctrine is based on the fact that evidence is actually discovered. That is, even if the police unlawfully enter a citizen's home, but later return with a warrant (based on information untainted by the unlawful entry) and conduct a search pursuant to that warrant, the with-warrant search is lawful because it was based on information from an *independent* source—independent of the unlawful entry.

HYPOTHETICAL

Police Chief Marck Jackson (hereafter "Chief Jackson") of the Fayetteberg Police Department found the following anonymous letter under his office door around 7:30 am on May 29, 2004:

> I am an employee at Wal-Market Super Center on 12th Street in Fayetteberg. You should know that several people on the Wal-Market management staff at this store are selling powdered cocaine to kids at Fayetteberg High School and Romney Jr. High. Two kids at Romney Jr. High died from overdosing on this toxic dope. The street name of this cocaine is "Triple H."
>
> By the way, some of these Wal-Market managers are quite well-known in the community. Two of them are named "Bob." You know them well! They brag on how they've made so much money selling drugs and how they can hide it through their regular jobs. They sell the cocaine from the employee restrooms at the 12th Street store. Most of the time Bob sells drugs from an apartment on Cleveland Street and Garland Avenue. When he sells from that apartment (#25), he is usually accompanied by a young man name Edwardo Gomez. Mr. Gomez usually carries the drugs and money for him. They also use the employee lockers to store (and sometimes sell from) the drugs. The drugs are sometimes stored in their cars.

Chief Jackson conducted a search of police files to determine if any students from Romney Jr. High had recently died of toxic drugs. After a two-hour search, he found records of three recent deaths by toxic drugs. Two of these deaths were of seventh graders at Canal Jr. High. The other death was of an eighth grader at Romney Jr. High. He also had several tips from reliable informants that "Bob" Sample sold drugs in the neighborhood.

After this search, Chief Jackson called the Wal-Market Home Office in Collierville. Chief Jackson identified himself and asked the appropriate personnel to locate the full name and address of the manager, "Jim Bob," at the 12th Street Super Center. After a ninety-minute search, the Home Office confirmed that there were two employee-managers at that store named "Bob." "Jim Bob" Sample was not only in his seventh year as a manager, but he was also a popular country-western singer in the Ozarks. Chief Jackson found hundreds of photographs depicting Bob Sample in advertisements for country and western shows throughout the Ozarks. James Robert ("Bob") Powell was a two-year veteran and a popular thespian in a local theater troupe. "Bob" Powell, however, was on duty at a Wal-Market in China.

Chief Jackson sent a team of six officers, led by Officer Frank Pendleton, to conduct a surveillance on the apartment (#25) at Cleveland Street and Garland Avenue. When Pendleton and his team arrived at apartment #25, they saw a woman crying hysterically as she ran from the apartment. The woman identified herself as Marcia Gomez, the wife of Edwardo Gomez, and joint lessee of apartment #25. She tearfully explained that when she returned to the apartment from her work as a dental hygienist, she found her husband, Edwardo, and two other men, Jose Ramirez and Alberto Ghia, lying dead on the living room floor. Before entering apartment #25, Officer Pendleton called for backup and emergency medical assistance. After these steps were taken, Officer Pendleton evacuated the building and "roped it off."

Inside apartment #25, Officer Pendleton and his police team found Edwardo and the two other victims lying face down on the floor with their hands tied behind their backs with zip ties. Each man had been shot in the back of the head at close range. Officer Pendleton's team also found almost ten kilos of cocaine in the apartment. They also found expended bullets and shell casings, and a cell phone on the floor next to Edwardo. One of the neighbors said that a man driving a red automobile was in the apartment when she heard shots being fired inside the apartment. She said she saw the red automobile parked in front of the building during the shooting. And then she saw it speed away immediately after the shooting.

The cell phone was traced to Edwardo's brother, Montel Gomez. Montel had been driving a truck in Montana during the time of the shooting. However, the police investigation of the numbers on the cell phone led them to Bob Sample's home at 2342 Dayton Place. When the police arrived at that address, they found a red automobile parked on the street in front of the house. The vanity plates on the automobile read "$Poket." The car was registered to Edwardo Gomez (of Fort Smith). Officer Pendleton approached a man and two women standing by the yard of 2342 Dayton Place. The man was Bob Sample, and the women were his mom, Catherine Sample and her best friend, Jo Anne Teague. Before Officer Pendleton could reach Sample in the yard he quickly walked toward them. He whispered to Pendleton that he was willing to talk to them but he wanted to do so at a place far away from his mom and her friend. Sample suggested that they talk at a nearby police station.

The officers took Sample to a nearby police station and interviewed him in a police interview room. The police neither videotaped Sample's statement nor read the familiar *Miranda* warnings to him. The door to the interview room remained open throughout the interview. Sample said that he had known Edwardo for several years and that they usually golfed at the Fayetteberg Country Club. Sample was a club member. Earlier that day he claimed that Edwardo and two of his friends drove up to play golf with him. Sample was informed at various times that he should not withhold any information, but should come clean with whatever he knew. Pendleton told him that they had phone records from a cell phone found in Apartment #25 at Cleveland and Garland that implicated him. After hearing about the cell phone, Sample claimed Edwardo wanted him to accompany him and his friends to an apartment on Cleveland Street and Garland Avenue. Edwardo was the driver, and he and the other two guys were passengers. Sample said he remained outside in the car while Edwardo and his two friends went inside. Once they were inside, Sample said he heard several shots come from inside the apartment. Sample said he panicked and drove away in the car as Edwardo had left the key in the ignition. The four officers did not comment on this story. Instead, they left Sample alone in the interview room.

Four hours later, six officers returned (including the four who were there earlier). This time Officer Pendleton read the familiar *Miranda* warnings to Sample. Sample made several incriminating statements. Two of those incriminating statements included his maybe entering the house and maybe shooting someone who charged him in a threatening way.

Defendant has filed a motion to exclude incriminating statements made during an interview at the police station as fruits of *Miranda*/Fifth Amendment violations. You are an associate prosecutor. Please provide your senior prosecutor with a memorandum of law: (1) analyzing the key legal precedents that the defendant will likely use to support his motions, (2) isolating the most persuasive arguments distilled from those precedents, and (3) predicting how the court is likely to rule on these competing arguments.

LIST OF READINGS

1. The Fifth Amendment to the United States Constitution.
2. The Sixth Amendment to the United States Constitution.
3. Federal Rules of Evidence Rule 401. Definition of Relevant Evidence.
4. Federal Rules of Evidence Rule 402. Relevant Evidence Generally Admissible; Irrelevant Evidence Inadmissible.
5. *Brown v. Mississippi*, 297 U.S. 278 (1936).
6. *Colorado v. Connelly*, 479 U.S. 157 (1986).
7. *Jackson v. Denno*, 378 U.S. 368 (1964).
8. *Crane v. Kentucky*, 476 U.S. 683 (1986).
9. *Ashcraft v. Tennessee*, 322 U.S. 143 (1944).
10. *Spano v. New York*, 360 U.S. 315 (1959).
11. *Payne v. Arkansas*, 356 U.S. 560 (1958).
12. *Arizona v. Fulminante*, 499 U.S. 279 (1991).
13. *Miranda v. Arizona*, 384 U.S. 436 (1966).
14. *Orozco v. Texas*, 394 U.S. 324 (1969).
15. *Minnesota v. Murphy*, 465 U.S. 420 (1984).
16. *Mathis v. United States*, 391 U.S. 1 (1968).
17. *Illinois v. Perkins*, 496 U.S. 292 (1990).
18. *Howes v. Fields*, 132 S. Ct. 1181 (2012).
19. *Berkermer v. McCarthy*, 468 U.S. 420 1984).
20. *Rhode Island v. Innis*, 446 U.S. 291 (1980).
21. *Pennsylvania v. Muniz*, 496 U.S. 582 (1990).
22. *Duckworth v. Eagan*, 492 U.S. 195 (1989).

23. *Florida v. Powell*, 130 S. Ct. 1195 (2010).
24. *Missouri v. Seibert*, 542 U.S. 600 (2004).
25. *Oregon v. Elstad*, 470 U.S. 298 (1985).
26. *Warden v. Dixon*, 132 S. Ct. 26 (2011).
27. *Michigan v. Tucker*, 417 U.S. 433 (1974).
28. *Chavez v. Martinez*, 538 U.S. 760 (2003).
29. *United States v. Patane*, 542 U.S. 630 (2004).
30. *New York v. Quarles*, 467 U.S. 649 (1984).
31. *Dickerson v. United States*, 530 U.S. 428 (2000).
32. *Harris v. New York*, 401 U.S. 222 (1971).
33. *Oregon v. Hass*, 420 U.S. 714 (1976).
34. *Doyle v. Ohio*, 426 U.S. 610 (1976).
35. *Jenkins v. Anderson*, 447 U.S. 231 (1980).
36. *Edwards v. Arizona*, 451 U.S. 477 (1981).
37. *North Carolina v. Butler*, 441 U.S. 369 (1969).
38. *Johnson v. Zerbst*, 304 U.S. 458 (1938).
39. *Davis v. United States*, 512 U.S. 452 (1994).
40. *Berghuis v. Thompkins*, 130 S. Ct. 2250 (2010).
41. *Arizona v. Roberson*, 486 U.S. 675 (1988).
42. *Minnick v. Mississippi*, 498 U.S. 146 (1990).
43. *Maryland v. Shatzer*, 130 S. Ct. 1213 (2010).
44. *Oregon v. Bradshaw*, 462 U.S. 1039 (1983).
45. *Texas v. Cobb*, 532 U.S. 162 (2001).
46. *Kirby v. Illinois*, 406 U.S. 682 (1972).
47. *Michigan v. Jackson*, 475 U.S. 625 (1986).
48. *Maine v. Moulton*, 474 U.S. 159 (1985).
49. *Massiah v. United States*, 377 U.S. 201 (1964).
50. *United States v. Henry*, 477 U.S. 264 (1980).
51. *Kuhlman v. Wilson*, 477 U.S. 436 (1986).
52. *Brewer v. Williams*, 430 U.S. 387 (1977).
53. *Nix v. Williams*, 467 U.S. 431 (1984).
54. *Murray v. United States*, 487 U.S. 533 (1988).
55. *McNeil v. Wisconsin*, 501 U.S. 171 (1991).
56. *Montejo v. Louisiana*, 556 U.S. 778 (2009).
57. Lawrence Herman, The Unexplored Relationship between the Privilege against Compulsory Self-Incrimination and the Involuntary Confession Rule (Part II), 53 Ohio St. L.J. 497 (1992).

SAMPLE ESSAY

To: Senior Prosecutor
From: Associate Prosecutor
Re: Suppression Hearing—State v. Sample
Defendant's Motion to Exclude incriminating statements made during an interview at the police station as fruits of *Miranda*/Fifth Amendment violations
Date:

In response to the motions-in-limine by the defendant that are described above, I have prepared the following memorandum of law for your consideration. As you will discover, this memorandum attempts to (1) identify the key legal precedents that the defendant uses to support his motions under the facts set out in the foregoing documents; (2) isolate the most persuasive arguments distilled from those precedents that he has asserted (and our counterargument to them); and (3) predict how the court is likely to rule on these competing arguments.

Essentially, the defendant will argue that (1) any statements he made during that first unwarned interrogation at the police station were fruits of a *Miranda* violation and should be excluded pursuant to the exclusionary rule, and (2) any statements he made after the second-warned interrogation should be excluded as well, because he claims that the statements made after the second-warned interrogation were tainted by the unconstitutional first interrogation. Neither argument survives applicable precedents.

First, Sample was not entitled to *Miranda*'s familiar warnings. Although he was subject to express interrogation, he was not in-custody for *Miranda* purposes. The *Miranda* Court held that, among other things, the familiar warnings must be given before a suspect makes the statements during custodial interrogation that the prosecutor wishes to be admitted into evidence. *Miranda* defined custodial interrogation as questioning initiated by law enforcement officers after a person has been taken into custody or otherwise deprived of his freedom of action in any significant way.

The Court has held in *California v. Beheler* that a citizen is not in-custody merely because he is questioned at the police station. And more recently the Court held in *Howes v. Fields* that even an incarcerated inmate who is interrogated about matters outside the prison walls is not necessarily in-custody for *Miranda* purposes. Indeed, the *Howes* Court opined that in order to determine whether an incarcerated inmate was in-custody for *Miranda* purposes, the court must take account of all the circumstances surrounding the interrogation. Pursuant to *Howes*, the court in our case should decide whether Sample was in-custody considering the totality of the circumstances.

Under the totality test factors indicating that he was not in-custody include (1) Sample asked the police to question him at a place other than his home, (2) the door to the interview room remained open throughout the interrogation, and (3) the police used no threats during the interrogation session. On the other hand, Sample has pointed to (1) the number of police in the room during the interrogation, (2) Officer Pendleton's encouraging him to clear things up, and (3) Officer Pendleton informing him that they had the phone records of a cell phone found in apartment #25.

After considering *Howes* and the totality of our facts, I believe the court will find that Sample was not in-custody for *Miranda* purposes. Thus, *Miranda* warnings were not required. Obviously, there is no *Miranda* violation if *Miranda* does not apply.

Second, Sample's second argument fails because it is dependent on a *Miranda* violation during the initial or unwarned interrogation. The Court has previously resolved the issue posed by the facts in our hypothetical: in *Missouri v. Seibert* the Court had to determine if any of a citizen's statements were admissible against him where he was first subjected to an unwarned custodial interrogation that was followed closely by a warned custodial interrogation. The Court held, in part, that where the subsequent warned interrogation appears to be a continuation of the unwarned interrogation, statements elicited from both interrogations were inadmissible. The subsequent or unwarned interrogation is usually considered a continuation of the first-unwarned interrogation if the interrogator at the subsequent interrogation draws a citizen's attention to what she said or how she said it during the first-unwarned interrogation.

The Court has, however, specifically held in *Oregon v. Elstad* that absent deliberately coercive or improper tactics in obtaining the initial statement, the mere fact that a suspect has made an unwarned statement does not indicate that he was coerced. In addition, the *Elstad* Court explained that providing *Miranda* warnings at the subsequent interrogation should not preclude admitting the subsequent statement. Our facts do not reveal that Officer Pendleton used any coercive tactics. Consequently, the incriminating statements produced at the subsequent warned interrogation should be admitted.

TOOLS FOR SELF-ASSESSMENT

Courts look at the totality of the circumstances surrounding an interrogation that lacks the required *Miranda* warnings. Custody is essential for the *Miranda* warnings to be mandatory. Determining whether Sample was in-custody under the totality of circumstances test when he was interrogated at the police station is not as clear as the prosecutor's essay suggests, primarily because the Court's articulation of its newly minted totality test has not been applied to our version of facts. Still, if the totality test can be applied to an incarcerated inmate, it would appear far less difficult to apply to a person who is merely questioned while in the station.

VARIATIONS OF THE THEME

Try the same problem, but this time, although Sample's statement is not videotaped and Sample does not receive the *Miranda* warnings, the door to the interrogation room is closed. Does this change the result?

TABLE OF CASES

TABLE OF CONSTITUTIONS, STATUTES, RULES, AND TREATIES

OTHER MATERIALS

Daniel Williams, Misplaced Angst: Another Look at Consent Search Jurisprudence, 82 Ind. L.J. 69 (Winter 2007).

Leslie A. Lunney, "Has the Fourth Amendment Gone to the Dogs? Unreasonable Expansion of Canine Sniff Doctrine to Include Sniff of the Home," 88 Or. L. Rev. 832–42 (2009).

Nancy J. Flatt-Moore, Public Schools and Urinalysis: Assessing the Validity of Indiana Public Schools Student Drug Testing Policies after *Vernonia*, 1998 B.Y.U. Educ. & L.J. 239, 252 (1998).

Note, You Say Yes, But Can I Say No?: The Future of Third-Party Consent Searches after *Georgia v. Randolph*, 73 Brook. L. Rev. 421 (2007).

Note: The Fourth Amendment and Antidilution: Confronting the Overlooked Function of the Consent Search Doctrine, 119 Harv. L. Rev. 2187 (2006).

Note: Third Party Consent Searches after *Georgia v. Randolph*: Dueling Approaches to the Dueling Roommates, 87 B.U. L. Rev. 937 (2007).

Orin S. Kerr, The Fourth Amendment and New Technologies: Constitutional Myths and the Case for Creation, 102 Mich. L. Rev. 709 (2004).

Peter P. Swire, Correspondence: Katz Is DEAD, Long Live Katz, 102 Mich. L. Rev. 904 (2004).

Robert D. Dodson, Ten Years of Randomized Jurisprudence: Amending the Special Needs Doctrine, 51 S.C. L. Rev. 258 (2000).

Ronald J. Allen et al., Criminal Procedure, Investigation and Right to Counsel, P.3 § C.1 The Probable Cause Standard 429 (2005).

Stephen A. Saltzburg, Another Victim of Illegal Narcotics: The Fourth Amendment (as Illustrated by the Open Fields Doctrine, 48 U. Pitt L. Rev. 1 (1986).

Survey. The Fourth Amendment, Password—Protected Computer Files and Third Party Consent Searches: The Tenth Circuit Broadens the Scope of Warrantless Searches, 85 Den. U. L. Rev. 701 (2008).

Yale Kamisar, Does (Did) (Should) the Exclusionary Rule Rest on a "Principled Basis" Rather than an Empirical Proposition"? 16 Creighton L. Rev. 565, 627–45 (1983).

Yale Kamisar, The "Automobile Search" Cases: The Court Does Little to Clarify the "Labyrinth" of Judicial Uncertainty, in 3 Supreme Court: Trends and Developments 1980–81, p. 69 (D. Opperman ed. 1982).

www.ingramcontent.com/pod-product-compliance
Ingram Content Group UK Ltd.
Pitfield, Milton Keynes, MK11 3LW, UK
UKHW050221160926
475595UK00015B/351

9 780199 795192